Imperfect Liberty

*A Defense of Those Rights
Endowed by Our Creator*

Scaevola

*"Malo periculosam,
libertatem quam quietam servitutem"*

- Thomas Jefferson

*"I should have loved freedom, I believe, at all times, but
in the time in which we live, I am ready to worship it."*

- Alexis de Tocqueville

Table of Contents

Author's Note

If you believe man has no inherent rights or free will, this work isn't intended to convince you otherwise. For the rest of us, it's a defense of natural rights—the core of American philosophy and our protection against centralized power. This information is presented as a guide meant to help you articulate your soul's inner voice, crying out that, yes, these rights are sacred and must be protected, even while the rest of the world views them as obstacles to "progress."

I have minimized commentary, focusing instead on summarizing and synthesizing a wealth of literature, philosophy, and history while trying not to oversimplify the issues. However, I had to strike a balance between approachability and verbosity. Also, the quotations contain many misspellings, but that's how they were written, and I elected to preserve the text as-is.

I bridge past and present by tracing the development of natural rights and highlighting, in their own words, the great minds who shaped the United States Constitution and our founding principles. Their fears, predictions, and concerns often speak directly to the societal challenges concerning rights, equality, and governance today.

That said, none of these figures were always correct in their opinions and assessments. Nor were they infallible, especially when judged through a modern lens. It's easy to criticize the past, benefitted by hindsight and contemporary morality. But how many of today's moral judges will have their own views challenged by future generations? Will that render their opinions and accomplishments meaningless? I should hope not.

Our Founders admitted that the Constitution was imperfect, yet figures like Frederick Douglass argued that its proper interpretation offers a brilliant path to liberty and equality. Unfortunately, power and greed have seized our government and economy, ushering them away from the Founders' intentions and placing us firmly within despotism's grasp.

What follows reflects much of my political philosophy—liberty through limited government—but I belong to no political party. My loyalty lies with individual liberty and truth, and I dedicate the following pages to those ideals.

Introduction

There are but two recognized sources of man's most sacred rights. They are either given and administered by the government, or they are inherent, bestowed upon him by his creator, and aren't subject to government infringement. The former has been the historical constant since the dawn of civilization. In every sense, the latter view caused the Declaration of Independence to be signed, the Revolutionary War to be fought, and the United States to be established.

While not always termed so, these "natural" rights have been rooted in natural law—universal, inherent moral principles discoverable through reason—since antiquity. Among others, the origins of natural rights can be traced back to the Greek philosopher Aristotle and the Roman orator Cicero, who argued that natural law is universal and binding on all humans. The concept became a working theory when it was expanded by the Christian theologian St. Thomas Aquinas.

Then, influenced by Aristotle, Aquinas, and later thinkers like Descartes, Newton, Bacon, Grotius, and Samuel von Pufendorf, Enlightenment Philosopher John Locke formalized these ideas into his theory of natural rights. He asserted that the right to life, liberty, and property stemmed from natural law and could be discovered through reason. He viewed these rights as intertwined, with each extending naturally into its practical applications.

For instance, life is a natural right, and man is justified in defending it against any threat. Liberty, essential to human dignity and self-determination, justifies rebellion against any tyrannical government that seeks to oppress it. Finally, property—comprising a man's self, his labor, and his wealth —forms the pillar of individual autonomy and the material foundation for his rights to life and liberty.

Contrary to some misguided beliefs, the United States Constitution doesn't grant these rights but was explicitly formed to protect them, proving that a fundamental distrust of government power lies at the heart of American philosophy. Indeed, the Constitution was designed to act as the government's shackles—not ours.

Liberty is the Basis

"Liberty is the basis—and whoever would dare to sap the foundation, or overturn the structure, under whatever specious pretexts he may attempt it, will merit the bitterest execration and the severest punishment which can be inflicted by his injured country." [1]

George Washington

The United States of America was born in rebellion against tyranny, forged in the fires of revolution, and ultimately founded on the radical ideals of liberty and self-government. America personified a latent spirit that had been trying to force its way into the forefront of human consciousness since the beginning of civilization itself—a spirit that yearns for freedom above slavery.

America's Founding Fathers believed no man was above righteous law, but at the same time, made every reasonable effort to ensure that the laws of men forever remained subordinate to our natural rights of life, liberty, and property. Those men believed that any degree of despotism was an unbearable burden upon their souls and must be thrown off in favor of liberty.

"All experience hath shewn," Thomas Jefferson wrote, "that mankind are more disposed to suffer, while evils are sufferable, than to right themselves by abolishing the forms to which they are accustomed. But when a long train of abuses and usurpations, pursuing invariably the same object evinces a design to reduce them under absolute despotism, it

---

[1] George Washington, Circular to the States, June 8, 1783.

is their right, it is their duty, to throw off such government, and to provide new guards for their future security."[2]

Our American Revolutionaries decreed that liberty was more important than security and servitude, squashing the antiquated notion of rights being handed down by men.

"Let us have a government," Washington demanded, "by which our lives, liberties, and properties will be secured."[3]

Jefferson clearly and concisely stated his position. "I would rather be exposed to the inconveniences attending too much liberty than those attending too small a degree of it."[4]

And yet, the evolution of a modern American aristocracy —a true relic of the past—has seized power and tries to convince us that the rest of the world was right all along. They say our Founders were morally and intellectually inferior and that society has "progressed" beyond their vision. They obfuscate the meaning of liberty and hope we forget that this ideal is the providential constant, no different today than in 1776.

If our founding premise was that all men are created equal, that's final. If men are endowed with inalienable natural rights, then those rights exist outside man's purview and control, and that's final. If the government derives its powers from the consent of the governed, then that's final. Where, then, can "progress" be found beyond equality and freedom? Or is it simply a deceptive regression to a time of less equality, fewer individual liberties, and pervasive tyranny?

This march toward despotism is nothing new, and our Founders took every precaution to delay it. As Benjamin

---

[2] Thomas Jefferson, The Declaration of Independence, July 4, 1776

[3] George Washington, Letter to Henry Lee, October 31, 1786.

[4] Thomas Jefferson, Letter to Archibald Stuart, December 23, 1791.

Franklin exited the Constitutional Convention on September 17, 1787, Mrs. Elizabeth Willing Powel asked, "Well, Doctor, what have we got, a republic or a monarchy?"

"A republic, if you can keep it,"[5] Franklin famously replied.

One look at the world's current state of affairs has many of us wondering if we can indeed keep it. And if so, how? It might seem idealistic, but the following solution was proposed by a man known for his pragmatism and insight—a man who aimed to provide a practical roadmap of power and statecraft but greatly admired the Roman Republic. "A return to first principles in a republic is sometimes caused by the simple virtues of one man, without depending upon any law that incites him to the infliction of extreme punishments; and yet his good example has such an influence that the good men strive to imitate him, and the wicked are ashamed to live a life so contrary to his example."[6]

Niccolò Machiavelli argued that the strength of a republic lies not just in its laws but in the moral character of those who uphold them. He supposed the Roman Republic might have endured had it consistently found leaders like Horatius Cocles, whose selfless courage defended Rome against its enemies; Fabricius Luscinus, an incorruptible paragon of virtue who placed the republic above personal gain; and Cato the Younger, who viciously opposed the rise of Caesar, revering the republic above all else.

In fact, the United States of America might not have existed at all if not for one such man's virtue. On Christmas Day, 1776, General Washington's army was in dire straits. Hoping to boost morale before a daring maneuver across the

---

[5] James McHenry, Journal of the Constitutional Convention, September 18, 1787.

[6] Niccolò Machiavelli, Discourses on Livy, 1517.

Delaware River, Washington shared the lines from a new pamphlet that had inspired him. "These are the times that try men's souls. The summer soldier and sunshine patriot will, in this crisis, shrink from the service of his country, but he that stands it now deserves the love and thanks of man and woman. Tyranny, like hell, is not easily conquered, yet we have this consolation with us—that the harder the conflict, the more glorious the triumph. What we obtain too cheap, we esteem too lightly: it is dearness only that gives everything its value. Heaven knows how to put a proper price upon its goods; and it would be strange indeed if so celestial an article as freedom should not be highly rated."[7]

Rejuvenated, Washington and his men fought and claimed victory at the Battle of Trenton, which proved to be a turning point in the Revolutionary War. After leading America to independence, General Washington surrendered his command and retired from public life, assuming his duty to America had been fulfilled.

The American people disagreed. Washington was seen as the only man who could unite the new republic and legitimize its government. Reluctantly, he listened and left Mount Vernon. "My movements to the chair of government will be accompanied by feelings not unlike those of a culprit who is going to the place of his execution; so unwilling am I, in the evening of a life nearly consumed in public cares, to quit a peaceful abode for an ocean of difficulties, without that competency of political skill—abilities—and inclination, which are necessary to manage the helm."[8]

---

[7] Thomas Paine, The American Crisis, No. 1, December 19, 1776, as read by General Washington on December 25th, 1776.

[8] George Washington, Letter to Henry Knox, March 1, 1789.

Three years later, President Washington had already become disillusioned with partisanship and political divide and attempted to escape public life once more. "The period for a new election of a citizen to administer the Executive Government of the United States being not far distant . . . I should now apprise you of the resolution I have formed, to decline being considered among the number of those out of whom a choice is to be made."[9]

Still, the American people demanded more from the man who had already given them everything. They, along with his cabinet and advisors, convinced Washington that his absence would create a power struggle and destabilize the country. Again, he listened, serving a second term and setting an example the subsequent seven two-term presidents would follow.

Thomas Jefferson emphasized the importance of setting such a precedent near the end of his second term. "If some termination to the services of the chief magistrate be not fixed by the Constitution, or supplied by practice, his office, nominally for years, will in fact, become for life . . . and I should unwillingly be the person who, disregarding the sound precedent set by an illustrious predecessor, should furnish the first example of prolongation beyond the second term of office."[10]

Similarly, James Madison, James Monroe, and Andrew Jackson wouldn't have dared seek a third term. Lincoln never had the opportunity. It wasn't until Ulysses S. Grant neared the end of his second term that a president seriously considered a third. However, public backlash put a stop to

---

[9] George Washington, Letter to Alexander Hamilton, May 1792.

[10] Thomas Jefferson, Letter to the Legislature of Vermont, December 10, 1807.

that idea. Grover Cleveland, the only president to date who served non-consecutive terms, had no interest in a third.

Woodrow Wilson likely would have been the first to seek a third term had his health not deteriorated rapidly, but Franklin Delano Roosevelt's poor health didn't prevent him from being the only president elected to third and fourth terms. That break from precedent led to the 22nd Amendment, limiting the presidency to two terms.

Perhaps Machiavelli was right after all. The simple virtues of one man—George Washington—and his good example had the power to influence generations of men. Yet, as time separates us from this example, his influence wanes. If we are to preserve our republic, we must rejuvenate it and return it to its first principles.

To do that, we need incorruptible men to stave off the moral decay synonymous with a fallen republic. We need men who understand that, though it might not be popular amongst a society taught to hate it, liberty is and will always be the basis of government for a free people. Otherwise, our fall, like Rome's, will forever be questioned and judged by history.

The United States Constitution

John Locke

When our Founding Fathers devised the United States Constitution, they drew inspiration, philosophy, and ideas from various sources to balance power, protect individual rights, and ensure government accountability.

For example, they considered Cicero's ideas on civic virtue[12], Rousseau's views on popular sovereignty[13], Blackstone's emphasis on the rule of law[14], and Montesquieu's thoughts on the separation of powers[15].

John Adams frequently referenced Algernon Sidney's works on liberty and republicanism in his defense of the United States Constitution. "As liberty consists only in being subjected to no man's will," Sidney wrote, "and nothing denotes a slave but a dependence upon the will of another; if there be no other law in a kingdom but the will of a prince, there is no such thing as liberty."[16]

These thinkers provided the foundational principles that guided the Constitution's Framers. Still, John Locke's theory

---

[11] John Locke, Two Treatises of Government, 1689.

[12] Cicero, On the Republic and On the Laws, 54-51 BC and 58-43 BC.

[13] Jean-Jacques Rousseau, The Social Contract, 1762.

[14] William Blackstone, Commentaries on the Laws of England, 1765-1769.

[15] Montesquieu, The Spirit of the Laws, 1748.

[16] Algernon Sidney, Discourses Concerning Government, 1698.

on natural rights and government by consent became the cornerstone of American political philosophy. Locke believed that government exists to protect the inherent rights of individuals, and once it failed to do so, it became illegitimate. "But if a long train of abuses, prevarications, and artifices, all tending the same way, make the design visible to the people, and they cannot but feel what they lie under, and see whither they are going; it is not to be wondered that they should then rouse themselves, and endeavor to put the rule into such hands which may secure to them the ends for which government was at first erected."[17]

Locke further warned of tyranny and described its catalyst. "Whenever the legislators endeavor to take away and destroy the property [18] of the people, or to reduce them to slavery under arbitrary power, they put themselves into a state of war with the people, who are thereupon absolved from any farther obedience." In this case, "The people have a right to resist and establish a new government when the old fails."[19]

Locke's principles were brought to life by Thomas Jefferson in the Declaration of Independence, where he explicitly articulated the people's right to overthrow a government that failed to protect their liberties. "We hold these truths to be self-evident, that all men are created equal, that they are endowed by their Creator with certain unalienable Rights, that among these are Life, Liberty and the pursuit of Happiness. That to secure these rights, Governments are instituted among Men, deriving their just powers from the consent of the governed, that whenever any

---

[17] John Locke, Two Treatises of Government, 1689.

[18] In this context, "property" refers to life, liberty, wealth, and possessions.

[19] John Locke, Two Treatises of Government, 1689.

Form of Government becomes destructive of these ends, it is the Right of the People to alter or to abolish it, and to institute new Government, laying its foundation on such principles and organizing its powers in such form, as to them shall seem most likely to effect their Safety and Happiness."[20]

Thus, the American Revolution was fought, and the United States of America was born with the establishment of our Constitution. James Madison, the "Father" of this new Constitution, stated its intended purpose. "Government is instituted to protect property of every sort; as well that which lies in the various rights of individuals, as that which the term particularly expresses. This being the end of government, that alone is a just government, which impartially secures to every man, whatever is his own."[21]

Our Founders believed that liberty is inherent—the natural state of mankind—and holds supremacy over government. Just as federal law supersedes local ordinances, natural rights stand above the Constitution, creating an elegant hierarchy whereby any infringement upon them is absolute despotism. However, without a bill of rights, Anti-Federalists argued that the original Constitution didn't go far enough to secure our liberties.

Noah Webster, Alexander Hamilton, James Madison, James Wilson, and other Federalists disagreed because, by design, the Constitution limited the federal government's powers to those expressly granted. Therefore, the government couldn't infringe on the individual rights it wasn't given the power to regulate in the first place.

---

[20] The Declaration of Independence, July 4, 1776.

[21] James Madison, Essay on Property, 1792.

Webster believed that enumerating rights in the Constitution would risk diminishing the importance of unlisted rights and imply that the government held dominion over them. "But let us not be deceived by the sound of words. A bill of rights may sound well to the uninformed, but what will be its use? It will exclude every thing that is not expressly mentioned, and leave it liable to dispute whether the legislature can pass any laws to enforce it."[22]

Hamilton went so far as to label a bill of rights as dangerous. "I go further, and affirm that bills of rights, in the sense and to the extent in which they are contended for, are not only unnecessary in the proposed Constitution, but would even be dangerous . . . Why declare that things shall not be done which there is no power to do?"[23]

James Wilson, one of the Constitution's Framers, said: "In the United States Constitution, it is declared that the powers not given are retained; and it says further, that no powers shall be exercised but what are expressly given. If we attempt to define the powers that we retain, we might enumerate all our rights, and there are certain residuary rights which we have never considered."[24]

George Mason, on the other hand, was a staunch advocate for a bill of rights. "There is no Declaration of Rights, and the laws of the general government being paramount to the laws and constitution of the several States, the Declarations of Rights in the separate States are no

---

[22] Noah Webster, A Citizen of America: An Examination Into the Leading Principles of America, October 17, 1787.

[23] Alexander Hamilton, Federalist No. 84, 1788.

[24] James Wilson, Speech during the Pennsylvania Ratifying Convention, October 6, 1787.

security. Nor are the people secured even in the enjoyment of the benefit of the common law."[25]

Patrick Henry was sure that, unless their rights were enumerated, the Federal Government would eventually devour those rights. "The necessity of a Bill of Rights appears to me to be greater in this Government, than ever it was in any Government before. I observed already, that the sense of the European nations, and particularly Great Britain, is against the construction of rights being retained, which are not expressly relinquished. I repeat, that all nations have adopted this construction—That all rights not expressly and unequivocally reserved to the people, are impliedly and incidentally relinquished to rulers; as necessarily inseparable from the delegated powers. It is so in Great Britain: For every possible right which is not reserved to the people by some express provision or compact, is within the King's prerogative."[26]

In a letter to Madison, Thomas Jefferson pointed out what he saw as the new Constitution's flaws, particularly "the omission of a bill of rights providing clearly & without the aid of sophisms for freedom of religion, freedom of the press, protection against standing armies . . . Let me add that a bill of rights is what the people are entitled to against every government on earth, general or particular, & what no just government should refuse or rest on inference."[27]

Ultimately, Madison changed his mind, and not only did he support the Bill of Rights, but he also played a pivotal role in crafting and gaining its adoption. In a speech to the House of Representatives, the future President described the

---

25 George Mason, Objections to This Constitution of Government, September 1787

26 Patrick Henry, Speech during the Virginia Convention, 16 June 1788.

27 Thomas Jefferson, Letter to James Madison, December 20, 1787.

proposed changes. "First. That there be prefixed to the Constitution a declaration, that all power is originally vested in, and consequently derived from, the people. That Government is instituted and ought to be exercised for the benefit of the people; which consists in the enjoyment of life and liberty, with the right of acquiring and using property, and generally of pursuing and obtaining happiness and safety . . . The people shall not be deprived or abridged of their right to speak, to write, or to publish their sentiments; and the freedom of the press, as one of the great bulwarks of liberty, shall be inviolable . . . the people shall not be restrained from peaceably assembling and consulting for their common good . . . the right of the people to keep and bear arms shall not be infringed,"[28] and so on.

In the more than 230 years since the Bill of Rights was ratified, the interpretation of its protections has deviated from the original intent. Debates over free speech, the right to bear arms, and privacy often hinge on the wording of their respective amendments rather than simply acknowledging them as fundamental rights with added protections.

This shift in perception—from seeing the Constitution as a document that absolutely limits government to one that defines individual rights—is a philosophical step backward toward antiquity and will only call forth those ancient tyrannies we thought were relegated to the past.

---

[28] James Madison, Speech in the House of Representatives, June 8, 1789.

The Right to Bear Arms

"This will not only lessen the call for military establishments, but if circumstances should at any time oblige the government to form an army of any magnitude that army can never be formidable to the liberties of the people while there is a large body of citizens, little, if at all, inferior to them in discipline and the use of arms, who stand ready to defend their own rights and those of their fellow citizens. This appears to me the only substitute that can be devised for a standing army, and the best possible security against it, if it should exist." [29]

Alexander Hamilton

America's Founding Fathers believed that certain rights and liberties are fundamental, inherent to human existence, and not subject to government decree. These rights, including the right to bear arms, are not "constitutional rights," nor are they predicated upon the existence of any amendment—they are perpetual and indispensable to preserving liberty.

That philosophy leads to an often-overlooked observation: even if the Second Amendment were repealed, our right to bear arms would not vanish with it. Instead, the government involved would expose itself as unjust, illegitimate, and dangerous for placing itself on our Creator's level by attempting to govern an expressly ungovernable right. In that event, armed resistance would not only be justified; it would become a duty, just as the Founders intended.

They recognized that an armed populace is an essential check on governmental power—a principle Aristotle

---

29 Alexander Hamilton, Federalist No. 29, January 9, 1789.

identified over 2,300 years ago: "For those who have the power of arms have the power to decide whether the constitution shall stand or fall."[30]

Perhaps Aristotle offered the most straightforward explanation behind a tyrant's attempt to disarm the people, and his reflection on the power of arms laid the groundwork for future thinkers to explore the moral and natural laws of armed men. The Roman statesman Cicero grounded the right to self-defense in natural law, a principle transcending manmade laws and institutions. He wrote, "There exists a law, not written down anywhere but inborn in our hearts; a law which comes to us not by training or custom or reading but from nature itself, if our lives are endangered, any and every method of protecting ourselves is morally right."[31]

Hugo Grotius, the 17th-century Dutch theologian, expanded upon the classical notion of natural law by integrating the right of individuals to resist oppression [32]. This provided the philosophical underpinnings of what John Locke would later refine into his natural rights theory.

Cesare Beccaria, influenced by Locke's views on the social contract, the right of revolution, and the Enlightenment's emphasis on reason and justice, applied these ideas to criminal justice. In his seminal work, *On Crimes and Punishments*, Beccaria argued against cruel and unusual punishment, advocating instead for a system where the certainty of punishment was prioritized over its severity. He strongly opposed laws that restricted individual freedoms, particularly those that infringed upon the right to self-defense, asserting that such laws not only failed to prevent

---

[30] Aristotle, Politics, 325-323 BC.
[31] Cicero, On the Laws, 58-43 BC.
[32] Hugo Grotius, On the Law of War and Peace, 1625.

crime but also exacerbated the conditions for injustice—a belief that largely impacted the opinions of Thomas Jefferson and James Madison.

Beccaria declared, "A principal source of errors and injustice are false ideas of utility. For example; that legislator has false ideas of utility, who considers particular more than general conveniences; who had rather command the sentiments of mankind than excite them, and dares say to reason, 'Be thou a slave;' who would sacrifice a thousand real advantages to the fear of an imaginary or trifling inconvenience; who would deprive men of the use of fire for fear of being burnt, and of water for fear of their being drowned; and who know of no means of preventing evil, but by destroying it. The laws of this nature, are those which forbid to wear arms, disarming those only who are not disposed to commit the crime which the laws mean to prevent . . . It certainly makes the situation of the assaulted worse, and the assailants better."[33]

Insights such as this shaped our Founders' understanding of liberty and rights. More specifically, they justified the American desire to break free from British rule and establish a government subordinate to the people. However, as discussed in the previous chapter, there was no consensus on how best to structure this new government, and the Constitution became the subject of heated debates.

Federalists advocated for a stronger central government, while Anti-Federalists favored decentralized power and additional protections for the liberties secured by the Revolution.

---

[33] Cesare Beccaria, On Crime and Punishment, 1764.

During this period, a series of letters published under the pseudonym "Federal Farmer" voiced concerns about the potential for government overreach. Likely written by Richard Henry Lee—a prominent Founding Father and Anti-Federalist—these letters emphasized the necessity of an armed populace to safeguard against tyranny. "It is true, the yeomanry of the country possess the lands, the weight of property, possess arms, and are too strong a body of men to be openly offended and, therefore, it is urged, they will take care of themselves, that men who shall govern will not dare pay any disrespect to their opinions."[34]

Seven days after Lee's letter, Noah Webster—a Federalist—published a pamphlet addressing the growing concerns surrounding the possibility of a federal standing army. Like Lee, he viewed an armed citizenry as the ultimate defense against despotism but rejected the notion of a military overpowering the people. "Before a standing army can rule, the people must be disarmed; as they are in almost every kingdom of Europe. The supreme power in America cannot enforce unjust laws by the sword; because the whole body of the people are armed, and constitute a force superior to any bands of regular troops that can be, on any pretense, raised in the United States."[35]

"A military force, at the command of Congress," Webster believed, "can execute no laws, but such as the people perceive to be just and constitutional; for [the people] will possess the power, and jealousy will instantly inspire the inclination, to resist the execution of a law which appears to

---

[34] Federal Farmer (Richard Henry Lee), Federal Farmer III, October 10, 1787.
[35] Noah Webster, A Citizen of America: An Examination Into the Leading Principles of America, October 17, 1787.

them unjust and oppressive."[36] In other words, Webster echoed Aristotle's idea that armed citizens control the fate of the Constitution.

Although Webster and Lee agreed on the importance of an armed citizenry, Lee had grave concerns about relying solely on the people to check a centralized military force. In "Federal Farmer XVIII," Richard Henry Lee countered Webster's dismissal of the dangers posed by a standing army or a select militia, warning that the Constitution must guard against establishing separate military forces. "First, the constitution ought to secure a genuine and guard against a select militia, by providing that the militia shall always be kept well organized, armed, and disciplined, and include, according to the past and general usuage of the states, all men capable of bearing arms; and that all regulations tending to render this general militia useless and defenceless, by establishing select corps of militia, or distinct bodies of military men, not having permanent interests and attachments in the community to be avoided. I am persuaded, I need not multiply words to convince you of the value and solidity of this principle, as it respects general liberty, and the duration of a free and mild government . . . this arrangement combines energy and safety in it; it places the sword in the hands of the solid interest of the community, and not in the hands of men destitute of property, of principle, or of attachment to the society and government."[37]

Lee concluded the same letter by reiterating the importance of all men being armed. "To preserve liberty, it is

---

[36] Noah Webster, A Citizen of America: An Examination Into the Leading Principles of America, October 17, 1787.

[37] Federal Farmer (Richard Henry Lee), Federal Farmer XVIII, January 25, 1788.

essential that the whole body of the people always possess arms and be taught alike, especially when young, how to use them."[38]

Less than a week later, James Madison contributed to the debate with *Federalist No. 46*. Like Noah Webster, Madison claimed that an armed populace would vastly outnumber any federal army. "The highest number to which, according to the best computation, a standing army can be carried in any country, does not exceed one hundredth part of the whole number of souls; or one twenty-fifth part of the number able to bear arms. This proportion would not yield, in the United States, an army of more than twenty-five or thirty thousand men. To these would be opposed a militia amounting to near half a million of citizens with arms in their hands, officered by men chosen from among themselves, fighting for their common liberties, and united and conducted by governments possessing their affections and confidence. It may well be doubted, whether a militia thus circumstanced could ever be conquered by such a proportion of regular troops."[39]

He then contrasted American ideals with European governments, emphasizing the unique duty placed on the American people. "Besides the advantage of being armed, which the Americans possess over the people of almost every other nation . . . the existence of [state] governments, to which the people are attached, and by which the militia officers are appointed, forms a barrier against the enterprises of ambition."[40] In Europe, Madison noted, governments feared arming their citizens, believing that

---

[38] Federal Farmer (Richard Henry Lee), Federal Farmer XVIII, January 25, 1788.

[39] James Madison, The Federalist No. 46, January 29, 1788.

[40] James Madison, The Federalist No. 46, January 29, 1788.

power should remain concentrated in the hands of rulers. "[Their] governments are afraid to trust the people with arms."[41]

While the debates between Federalists and Anti-Federalists intensified, it's important to point out that both sides were committed to protecting the right to bear arms, free speech, and other fundamental liberties; they only differed on how best to safeguard them. Federalists trusted that the Constitution's enumerated powers and checks and balances would be enough to prevent tyranny. However, the Anti-Federalists remained unconvinced, fearing that more explicit protections were necessary.

On February 6th, 1788, Samuel Adams introduced a motion at the Massachusetts Ratifying Convention that aimed to clarify and strengthen Constitutional limits, demanding "that the said Constitution never be construed to authorize Congress to infringe the just liberty of the press, or the rights of conscience; or to prevent the people of the United States, who are peaceful citizens, from keeping their own arms."[42]

Later, at the Virginia Ratifying Convention, Patrick Henry passionately predicted disaster if the Constitution wasn't amended to include more security for Americans' rights. "Guard with jealous attention the public liberty. Suspect every one who approaches that jewel. Unfortunately, nothing will preserve it but downright force. Whenever you give up that force, you are inevitably ruined."[43]

---

41 James Madison, The Federalist No. 46, January 29, 1788.

42 Samuel Adams, Speech at the Massachusetts Ratifying Convention, February 6, 1788.

43 Patrick Henry, Speech at the Virginia Ratifying Convention, June 1788.

Henry, remembered for his Revolutionary Era ultimatum, "Give me liberty, or give me death,"[44] saw the dangers of placing militia control in the central government's hands. How could men protect their liberties if their defense was only secured by the very government they feared? "My great objection to this government is, that it does not leave us the means of defending our rights, or of waging war against tyrants. It is urged by some gentlemen, that this new plan will bring us an acquisition of strength—an army, and the militia of the states. This is an idea extremely ridiculous: gentlemen cannot be earnest. This acquisition will trample on our fallen liberty. Let my beloved Americans guard against that fatal lethargy that has pervaded the universe. Have we the means of resisting disciplined armies, when our only defence, the militia, is put into the hands of Congress?"[45]

The foundation of our Constitutional structure rests on the separation of powers and checks and balances to prevent any one branch of government from becoming too powerful. Yet, without an armed citizenry acting as a check on the government, what good are checks and balances within that government? For this reason, as evidenced above and supported by Hamilton's quote to open this chapter, Americans are not merely meant to be armed; they're expected to be armed to such a degree that they pose a formidable threat to any potential tyranny—foreign or domestic.

Patrick Henry proceeded to challenge the more optimistic assumptions of Webster and Madison. "The honorable gentleman who presides told us that, to prevent abuses in

---

[44] Patrick Henry, Speech at the Second Virginia Convention, March 23, 1775.

[45] Patrick Henry, Speech at the Virginia Ratifying Convention, June 1788.

our government, we will assemble in Convention, recall our delegated powers, and punish our servants for abusing the trust reposed in them. O sir, we should have fine times, indeed, if, to punish tyrants, it were only sufficient to assemble the people! Your arms, wherewith you could defend yourselves, are gone; and you have no longer an aristocratical, no longer a democratical spirit. Did you ever read of any revolution in a nation, brought about by the punishment of those in power, inflicted by those who had no power at all? You read of a riot act in a country which is called one of the freest in the world, where a few neighbors cannot assemble without the risk of being shot by a hired soldiery, the engines of despotism. We may see such an act in America. A standing army we shall have, also, to execute the execrable commands of tyranny; and how are you to punish them? Will you order them to be punished? Who shall obey these orders? Will your mace-bearer be a match for a disciplined regiment?"[46]

George Mason also attended the Virginia Ratifying Convention and warned that all men must be armed to prevent the militia from becoming an exclusive, standing force. He didn't want America to transform into Germany or Prussia, where the select militia served as the ruling class' tool of oppression. "A worthy member has asked who are the militia, if they be not the people of this country, and if we are not to be protected from the fate of the Germans, Prussians, &c., by our representation? I ask, Who are the militia? They consist now of the whole people, except a few public officers. But I cannot say who will be the militia of the future day. If that paper on the table [the Constitution] gets no alteration,

---

46 Patrick Henry, Speech at the Virginia Ratifying Convention, June 1788.

the militia of the future day may not consist of all classes, high and low, and rich and poor; but they may be confined to the lower and middle classes of the people, granting exclusion to the higher classes of the people."[47]

After ratification but before the Bill of Rights was adopted, George Washington summed up the importance of a self-sufficient and well-armed populace during his First Annual Address. "A free people ought not only to be armed but disciplined; to which end a uniform and well-digested plan is requisite: and their safety and interest require that they should promote such manufactories as tend to render them independent on others for essential, particularly military, supplies."[48]

Thomas Jefferson later added, "The Greeks and Romans had no standing armies, yet they defended themselves. The Greeks by their laws, and the Romans by the spirit of their people, took care to put into the hands of their rulers no such engine of oppression as a standing army. Their system was to make every man a soldier, and oblige him to repair to the standard of his country whenever that was reared. This made them invincible; and the same remedy will make us so."[49]

We've established that arguments against the right to bear arms are critically flawed. It's an inviolable natural right, not contingent upon the Second Amendment for its existence. Moreover, "militia" was inarguably understood to mean "all able-bodied citizens" rather than a governmental force. Yet, calls for restrictions based on the phrase "well regulated" persist.

---

[47] George Mason, Speech at the Virginia Ratifying Convention, June 1788.

[48] George Washington, First Annual Address, To Both Houses of Congress, January 8, 1790.

[49] Thomas Jefferson, Letter to Thomas Cooper, September 10, 1814.

"Well regulated" in the 18th-century context didn't mean government-imposed restrictions. Instead, it referred to something being in proper working order or well-trained. Numerous documents from that era confirm this definition, including James Madison's own notes from the Federal Convention.[50]

This interpretation has been legally affirmed in the 21st century as well. In the landmark Supreme Court case, "District of Columbia v. Heller, Justice Antonin Scalia wrote for the majority, "The adjective 'well regulated' implies nothing more than the imposition of proper discipline and training."[51]

I could continue defending the Second Amendment's text and historical context, but doing so ultimately distracts from the inherent truth: the Founding Fathers left behind no ambiguity, and any attempt to reinterpret these rights for "modern society" only distances us from America's core principles.

In modern society, though, the prevalence of gun crime is often cited as a "legitimate" objection against the right to bear arms. However, gun crime isn't an indictment on the right itself; it's a reflection of broader societal and governmental failures—particularly those in law enforcement and justice. When laws fail and the state doesn't punish swiftly and equally, a republican government loses its ability to maintain order, just as Montesquieu observed. "When, in a popular government, there is a suspension of the laws, as this can proceed only from the corruption of the republic, the state is certainly undone."[52]

---

50 James Madison, Notes on the Federal Convention, 1787.

51 Antonin Scalia, District of Columbia v. Heller, 554 U.S. 570 2008.

52 Montesquieu, The Spirit of the Laws, 1748.

Rather than addressing the systemic issues at the root of the problem, our liberties are blamed, and the Second Amendment is attacked to cover up negligence and corruption. As Beccaria and other Enlightenment thinkers knew, liberty should never be sacrificed for the false promise of security. Doing so merely leaves us vulnerable to criminal and governmental tyranny.

As "progressive" ideologies shift away from our Founding philosophy, our rights are increasingly labeled a "threat to democracy." Meanwhile, our Chief Magistrate demonstrated a willingness to wield military force against his own people, just as the Anti-Federalists feared—"a threat to the republic," the Founders might warn.

President Joe Biden said, "And for those brave right-wing Americans who say [the Second Amendment] is all about keeping America independent and safe, if you want to fight against the country, you need an F-15. You need something more than a gun."[53] Months later, he doubled down: "If you need to worry about taking on the federal government, you need some F-15s. You don't need an AR-15."[54]

King George III might have argued that Americans would have needed the world's strongest navy to compete with Britain, too. While Biden's comments were fundamentally anti-American, they were a symptom of a more significant problem. They suggested that the government no longer fears offending its people, a stark departure from Webster, Hamilton, and Madison's vision.

Perhaps the more chilling implication, however, is that a right could be determined obsolete by the very power it was designed to check. If we permit the government to redefine

---

53 President Joe Biden, Speech in Wilkes-Barre, Pennsylvania, August 30, 2022.

54 President Joe Biden, Speech on National Action Network, January 16, 2023.

or disregard rights based on perceived utility, then no right is genuinely safe.

Perhaps the applause Biden received was as troubling as the statements themselves. In their eagerness to support their leader, the crowd failed to realize that his threats, although aimed at so-called "right-wing Americans," affect us all. Without geographical boundaries, missiles or bombs don't distinguish between party lines or ideologies. Everyone is at risk. I suppose Biden wished to remind us of a historical maxim: tyrants with armies protect the tyrant; citizens with arms protect their liberty.

Freedom of Speech

"If all mankind minus one were of one opinion, and only one person were of the contrary opinion, mankind would be no more justified in silencing that one person than he, if he had the power, would be justified in silencing mankind . . . We can never be sure that the opinion we are endeavouring to stifle is a false opinion; and if we were sure, stifling it would be an evil still." [55]

John Stuart Mill

I began this section on rights with the right to bear arms for a reason. As perhaps the most controversial of our rights, it provided a fitting foundation to discuss the core principles of liberty. The same arguments that Enlightenment thinkers and our Founders used to defend the right to bear arms— that it is natural, ungovernable, and intrinsic—apply equally to the freedom of speech. Just as the right to bear arms is not contingent upon any amendment, neither is the right to think, speak, or write one's opinions freely. Therefore, laboring over a defense of free speech's inherent necessity seems unnecessary. Instead, I choose to apply that energy toward its preservation.

Are there limits to free speech? And if so, where is that proverbial red line between freedom and restriction? I, along with others who are much more intelligent than myself, argue there are no limitations on man's natural rights—at least, not on the rights themselves. There is, however, a distinction between right and license, as John Locke noted. "But though this be a state of liberty, yet it is not a state of

---

55 John Stuart Mill, On Liberty, 1859.

licence . . . being all equal and independent, no one ought to harm another in his life, health, liberty, or possessions."[56]

In other words, one man's rights do not grant him the license to infringe on another man's life, health, liberty, or possessions. For example, the right to bear arms protects man from threats to physical safety and freedom, but that right doesn't include the license to cause unprovoked harm to others. Likewise, free speech protects man and society from intellectual and political tyranny but doesn't allow him to attack another's livelihood with provable lies.

Benjamin Franklin echoed Locke's sentiments. "Without Freedom of Thought, there can be no such Thing as Wisdom; and no such Thing as publick Liberty, without Freedom of Speech; which is the Right of every Man, as far as by it, he does not hurt or controul the Right of another: And this is the only Check it ought to suffer, and the only Bounds it ought to know . . . Whoever would overthrow the Liberty of a Nation, must begin by subduing the Freeness of Speech."[57]

In the mid-1800s, English philosopher John Stuart Mill expanded on these ideas with *On Liberty*. In this highly influential text on individual liberty and free speech, Mill argued that individuals should be free to act as they wish, provided that their actions—apart from self-defense—do not harm others in any measurable way. Mill's "Harm Principle" became an invaluable tool to distinguish free speech from righteously restricted speech. "The sole end for which mankind are warranted, individually or collectively, in interfering with the liberty of action of any of their number, is self-protection . . . His own good, either physical or moral, is not a sufficient warrant. He cannot rightfully be compelled

---

56 John Locke, Two Treatises of Government, 1689.

57 Benjamin Franklin, Silence Dogood, No. 8, July 9, 1722.

to do or forbear because it will be better for him to do so, because it will make him happier, because, in the opinions of others, to do so would be wise, or even right. These are good reasons for remonstrating with him, or reasoning with him, or persuading him, or entreating him, but not for compelling him, or visiting him with any evil in case he do otherwise . . . the only freedom which deserves the name, is that of pursuing our own good in our own way, so long as we do not attempt to deprive others of theirs, or impede their efforts to obtain it. Each is the proper guardian of his own health, whether bodily, or mental and spiritual. Mankind are greater gainers by suffering each other to live as seems good to themselves, than by compelling each to live as seems good to the rest."[58]

Therein lies the heart of modernity's free speech debate: harm. Groups and governments worldwide are increasing their calls to limit speech under the guise of protecting society from harm. But what constitutes measurable harm as a result of words? More importantly, who defines harm? And who holds the measuring stick?

In the 21st century, "harm" has been stretched to include subjective grievances, hurt feelings, speaking out against the government, and ideological disagreements rather than calculable injury. This is opposed to free speech's fundamental purpose, which is precisely to challenge or criticize the evolution of ideas and morality. What was once understood as a tool for protecting men from authoritarianism is now being reshaped to justify censorship in the name of comfort and conformity.

---

[58] John Stuart Mill, On Liberty, 1859.

The English poet John Milton, best known for his epic poem, *Paradise Lost,* gave one of history's most passionate defenses of free speech in *Areopagitica.* Vehemently opposed to censorship, he argued that exposure to lies and errors is necessary for growth, while censorship and force undermine this process. "Let [Truth] and Falsehood grapple; who ever knew Truth put to the worse, in a free and open encounter . . . Truth is strong next to the Almighty; she needs no policies, nor stratagems, nor licencings to make her victorious."[59]

It's easy to champion free speech when most expressed opinions align with one's own. But in the social media age, dissidents are often attacked, ostracized, or subjected to being "canceled," so they stay quiet. Worse, people are being persecuted and prosecuted for merely voicing their "hateful" or "misinformed" views as determined by the arbitrary will of others. Yet, much of the world seems to have no problem with this censorship, considering it a reasonable consequence of "wrongthink," and are quick to declare, "Not all speech is free speech."

Free speech demands engagement—not punishment for dissent—and truth doesn't need protection from "misinformation" or even outright lies. In fact, if misinformation could be proven false, it would be called a lie, and to call anything "misinformation" is itself a form of propaganda. When a man can express his opinions—no matter how offensive—worship his own god and assemble peacefully, power rests with the people. When we censor discussion, we take away that power with an assumption of

---

[59] John Milton, Areopagitica, 1644.

infallibility, and only a tyrant confuses *his* certainty with absolute certainty.

However, tyranny doesn't always present itself as a single authoritarian. "When society is itself the tyrant," John Stuart Mill said, "society collectively, over the separate individuals who compose it—its means of tyrannizing are not restricted to the acts which it may do by the hands of its political functionaries. Society can and does execute its own mandates: and if it issues wrong mandates instead of right, or any mandates at all in things with which it ought not to meddle, it practises a social tyranny more formidable than many kinds of political oppression, since, though not usually upheld by such extreme penalties, it leaves fewer means of escape, penetrating much more deeply into the details of life, and enslaving the soul itself. Protection, therefore, against the tyranny of the magistrate is not enough: there needs protection also against the tyranny of the prevailing opinion and feeling; against the tendency of society to impose, by other means than civil penalties, its own ideas and practices as rules of conduct on those who dissent from them; to fetter the development, and, if possible, prevent the formation, of any individuality not in harmony with its ways, and compel all characters to fashion themselves upon the model of its own."[60]

Harm's best litmus test is that of subjective versus objective harm. Subjective harm refers to emotional distress or offense, which varies widely based on personal feelings and thresholds. What one individual finds offensive may not affect another similarly, making it impossible to measure universally. Objective harm involves direct, provable impacts

---

[60] John Stuart Mill, On Liberty, 1859.

or threats to an individual's life, liberty, or property. This includes cases like slander or defamation, where the harm is concrete and can be demonstrated through evidence, such as financial loss, damage to reputation, or physical harm.

There are exceptions to this litmus test. Minors and those with cognitive disabilities or mental health disorders require protection from their actions and external harm, given that they do not possess the faculties necessary for sound judgment. "It is, perhaps, hardly necessary to say that this doctrine is meant to apply only to human beings in the maturity of their faculties," Mill wrote. "We are not speaking of children, or of young persons below the age which the law may fix as that of manhood or womanhood. Those who are still in a state to require being taken care of by others, must be protected against their own actions as well as against external injury."[61]

And what of incitement to insurrection or violence? Is that free speech? In short, the harm principle applies to people—not the state. Following in the tradition of Locke and Mill, a citizen's incitement to violence against other citizens is not free speech because, in part, it establishes an actionable threat of objective harm. However, a citizen's outspoken critique of the state, which a despotic government might be inclined to define as "incitement to insurrection or rebellion," is, perhaps, the most vital function of free speech.

It follows that the reverse is also true: the government has no right to sway public opinion through collusion with the media or other information sources. Mill argued this to be self-evident. "No argument, we may suppose, can now be needed, against permitting a legislature or an executive, not

---

61 John Stuart Mill, On Liberty, 1859.

identified in interest with the people, to prescribe opinions to them, and determine what doctrines or what arguments they shall be allowed to hear."[62]

President Calvin Coolidge agreed, warning, "Wherever despotism abounds, the sources of public information are the first to be brought under its control . . . The public press under an autocracy is necessarily a true agency of propaganda. Under a free government, it must be the very reverse."[63]

Benjamin Franklin wrote, "Only the wicked Governours of Men dread what is said of them . . . Freedom of Speech is ever the Symptom, as well as the Effect of a good Government."[64] He then cited Rome's Horatius, Valerius, Cincinnatus, and other virtuous leaders who had nothing to fear from liberty of speech. He stated that the more their administrations were examined, the more their administrations became enlightened. That is until Rome's liberty began to fade. "But Things afterwards took another Turn. Rome, with the Loss of its Liberty, lost also its Freedom of Speech; then Mens Words began to be feared and watched; and then first began the poysonous Race of Informers."[65]

These "informers" Franklin spoke of were incentivized by power and the possibility of gaining favor with the government by betraying their fellow citizens. Their actions led to a culture of fear and repression, as even harmless statements could be twisted into offenses against the state. To prevent such tyranny, men must habitually criticize the

---

[62] John Stuart Mill, On Liberty, 1859.

[63] Calvin Coolidge, The Press Under a Free Government, January 17, 1925.

[64] Benjamin Franklin, Silence Dogood No. 8, July 9, 1722.

[65] Benjamin Franklin, Silence Dogood No. 8, July 9, 1722.

state, checking its lust for power. For, if a state has no power or favors to offer, "informers" have no place within it.

Following Shay's Rebellion[66] and influenced by France's growing revolutionary sentiments, Thomas Jefferson concluded that righteous rebellion was a necessary public action to hold the government accountable and prevent the encroachment of rights. "I hold it, that a little rebellion, now and then, is a good thing, and as necessary in the political world as storms in the physical. Unsuccessful rebellions, indeed, generally establish the encroachments on the rights of the people, which have produced them. An observation of this truth should render honest republican governors so mild in their punishment of rebellions, as not to discourage them too much. It is a medicine necessary for the sound health of government."[67]

A few months later, Jefferson mentioned Shay's Rebellion again. "Can history produce an instance of rebellion so honorably conducted? I say nothing of its motives. They were founded in ignorance, not wickedness. God forbid we should ever be twenty years without such a rebellion. The people cannot be all, and always, well informed. The part which is wrong will be discontented, in proportion to the importance of the facts they misconceive. If they remain quiet under such misconceptions, it is a lethargy, the forerunner of death to the public liberty."[68]

Upon reading the proposed Constitution, Jefferson was concerned that the Constitutional Convention had been overly affected by Shay's Rebellion and granted too much

---

[66] Shay's Rebellion: an armed uprising in 1786-87 led by Revolutionary War veteran Daniel Shays, where disgruntled Massachusetts farmers protested economic injustices and oppressive debt collection, highlighting the weaknesses of the Articles of Confederation.

[67] Thomas Jefferson, Letter to James Madison, Paris, January 30, 1787.

[68] Thomas Jefferson, Letter to Colonel Smith, Paris, November 13, 1787.

power to the federal government. In the same letter, he wrote one of his most cited thoughts. "What country can preserve its liberties, if its rulers are not warned from time to time, that this people preserve the spirit of resistance? Let them take arms. The remedy is to set them right as to facts, pardon and pacify them. What signify a few lives lost in a century or two? The tree of liberty must be refreshed from time to time, with the blood of patriots and tyrants. It is its natural manure."[69]

Just over a decade later, John Adams confirmed Jefferson's fears of an overzealous government by signing the Alien and Sedition Acts into law amid growing tensions with France. The Sedition Act made it illegal to criticize the government. While Adams argued it was due to national security concerns, the Sedition Act blurred the line between dissent and rebellion. In essence, it branded negative opinions of the young government as potential incitements to insurrection, exemplifying the inherent danger of allowing the government to define "incitement" as spoken by its citizens.

Among many others, James Madison and Thomas Jefferson fiercely opposed Adams' seizure of powers not delegated in the Constitution. Jefferson fought against the President, drafting the Kentucky Resolutions of 1798. "No power over the freedom of religion, freedom of speech, or freedom of the press being delegated to the US. by the constitution, nor prohibited by it to the states, all lawful powers respecting the same did of right remain, & were reserved, to the states or the people."[70]

---

[69] Thomas Jefferson, Letter to Colonel Smith, Paris, November 13, 1787.
[70] Thomas Jefferson, Letter to James Madison with Kentucky Resolution Enclosure, November 17, 1798.

Jefferson warned that these acts swept away constitutional barriers and made "outlaws" of peaceable inhabitants who might one day venture to reclaim their rights. He even had a legitimate fear that these acts, "Unless arrested at the threshold, necessarily drive these states into revolution & blood, & will furnish new calumnies against republican government, & new pretexts for those who wish it to be believed that man cannot be governed but by a rod of iron."[71]

Trust in government, Jefferson asserted, is the parent of despotism, and a healthy distrust (jealousy) of "men of our choice" (elected officials) is a proper and necessary check on authority. "It would be a dangerous delusion, were a confidence in the men of our choice to silence our fears for the safety of our rights; that confidence is every where the parent of despotism; free government is founded in jealousy, and not in confidence."[72]

Having read Jefferson's Kentucky draft, Madison wrote the Virginia Resolutions of 1798, similarly condemning President Adams, albeit with a more measured tone. Madison even contended that free speech is the only effectual guardian of every other right. "That the General Assembly doth particularly protest against the palpable and alarming infractions of the constitution . . . [which] exercises in like manner a power not delegated by the constitution, but on the contrary expressly and positively forbidden by one of the amendments thereto; a power which more than any other ought to produce universal alarm, because it is levelled

---

[71] Thomas Jefferson, Letter to James Madison with Kentucky Resolution Enclosure, November 17, 1798.

[72] Thomas Jefferson, Letter to James Madison with Kentucky Resolution Enclosure, November 17, 1798.

against that right of freely examining public characters and measures, and of free communication among the people thereon, which has ever been justly deemed, the only effectual guardian of every other right."[73]

Madison cautioned against the established precedent, invoking the conditions upon which Virginia ratified the Constitution, demanded additional protections in the Bill of Rights, and entered the United States. "This State having by its convention which ratified the federal constitution, expressly declared, 'that among other essential rights, the liberty of conscience and of the press cannot be cancelled, abridged, restrained or modified by any authority of the United States' and from its extreme anxiety to guard these rights from every possible attack of sophistry or ambition, having with other states recommended an amendment for that purpose, which amendment was in due time annexed to the Constitution, it would mark a reproachful inconsistency and criminal degeneracy, if an indifference were now shewn to the most palpable violation of one of the rights thus declared and secured, and to the establishment of a precedent which may be fatal to the other."[74]

President Adams' Alien and Sedition Acts played a role in Jefferson's decision to seek the presidency and Adams' eventual defeat. Upon entering office in 1801, Jefferson immediately took the necessary steps to dismantle the laws. The Sedition Act expired, and Jefferson pardoned the convicted, remitted their fines, and ensured the acts would not be enforced during his presidency.

This clash between what Adams perceived as necessary national protections and the opposition's defense of free

---

[73] James Madison, The Virginia Resolutions, 1798.

[74] James Madison, The Virginia Resolutions, 1798.

speech—led by the man who authored the Constitution and Bill of Rights—reveals an unsettling truth: the United States Government will overstep its authority and limit speech to serve its own interests, even under questionable pretenses.

Yet, we're asked to give it more power to control speech for "our protection." Even if our government were that utopian version of republicanism where civic virtue and morality flowed unimpeded from the wellspring of human hearts and earned our unwavering trust, granting them this privilege would still be unwise because the freedom of speech is not theirs to govern.

A government, or even a society that fears or suppresses open discourse, isn't a steward of liberty; they are its bane. Ultimately, speech should only be restricted when it is directly and demonstrably intended to cause imminent, specific, and actionable harm to life, liberty, or property.

Property Rights

"Property, not conscience, is the basis of liberty. For the defense of conscience need not arise. Property is always exposed to interference. It is the constant object of policy." [75]

Lord John Dalberg-Acton

While we tend to think of "property" in terms of land, historically, the concept includes personal property, real estate, and financial assets. During the Enlightenment, John Locke played a pivotal role in broadening the definition of property to include life and liberty. Since then, property has been understood as the foundation of personal freedom and autonomy, essential to the individual's ability to act independently of external control.

The two opposing schools of thought in Western philosophy regarding property can be traced to two men: Plato and Aristotle. Plato advocated for communal property, emphasizing collective ownership to reduce conflict and promote social unity. His pupil, Aristotle, had drastically different views, arguing that private property encouraged individual virtue and led to a more harmonious society by aligning responsibility with ownership.

Perhaps among the first to link private property with individual well-being and societal progress, Aristotle wrote, "Property should be in a certain sense common, but, as a general rule, private; for, when every one has a distinct interest, men will not complain of one another, and they will make more progress, because every one will be attending to

---

[75] Lord Acton, History of Freedom and Other Essays, 1907.

his own business."[76] For Aristotle, property wasn't just an economic asset but necessary for responsible citizenship.

Following the Greek tradition, Cicero grounded his understanding of property in natural law. In his view, private property was fundamental to the righteous existence of governments, which should be designed to protect individual ownership. He also warned that undermining private property through confiscation or other injustices could destabilize the republic, leading to despotism. "[Philippus'] speech[77] deserves unqualified condemnation, for it favoured an equal distribution of property; and what more ruinous policy than that could be conceived? For the chief purpose in the establishment of constitutional state and municipal governments was that individual property rights might be secured."[78]

In the medieval era, the Italian philosopher and theologian St. Thomas Aquinas suggested a stronger bond between property rights, Christian principles, and natural law. Drawing heavily from Aristotle and Christian theology, Aquinas maintained that ownership is a natural extension of man's ability to provide for himself and organize society. In response to objections against private ownership, Aquinas wrote, "Two things are competent to man in respect of exterior things. One is the power to procure and dispense them, and in this regard it is lawful for man to possess property. Moreover, this is necessary to human life for three reasons. First, because everyone is more careful to procure what is for himself alone than that which is common to many

---

76 Aristotle, Politics, 325-323 BC.

77 Lucius Marcius Philippus, Speech advocating a law that would redistribute land to address wealth inequality in Rome, 104 BC.

78 Cicero, On the Laws, 58-43 BC.

or to all: since each one would shirk the labor and leave to another that which concerns the community, as happens where there is a great number of servants. Secondly, because human affairs are conducted in a more orderly fashion if each man is charged with taking care of some particular thing himself, whereas there would be confusion if everyone had to look after any one thing indeterminately. Thirdly, because a more peaceful state is ensured to man if each one is contented with his own."[79]

Like Aristotle, Aquinas believed private property was integral to fostering personal responsibility and social order, but he also asserted property comes with moral obligations. "The second thing that is competent to man with regard to external things is their use. In this respect, man ought to possess external things, not as his own, but as common, so that, to wit, he is ready to communicate them to others in their need."[80]

Hugo Grotius later argued that all things were held in common in nature, but individuals could appropriate property through their labor and occupation. [81] Samuel von Pufendorf, a 17th-century German philosopher and legal theorist, regarded private property as essential for peace, prosperity, and cooperation.[82]

Grotius and Pufendorf's works, in particular, helped shape John Locke's more elaborate and individualistic theory of property rights. Locke believed that property was a natural right, stemming from an even more fundamental ownership—the ownership of oneself—and was the first to

---

[79] St. Thomas Aquinas, *Summa Theologica*, 1265-1274.
[80] St. Thomas Aquinas, *Summa Theologica*, 1265-1274.
[81] Hugo Grotius, On the Law of War and Peace, 1625.
[82] Samuel von Pufendorf, On the Law of Nature and Nations, 1672.

connect property to liberty systematically. "Property includes a man's life, liberty, and possessions . . . every man has a property in his own person: this no body has any right to but himself. The labour of his body, and the work of his hands, we may say, are properly his."[83]

This notion was revolutionary in the late 17th-century Europe. Land and property were primarily concentrated within the ruling class or monarchy, and most people had little or no control over it. Locke challenged this system by asserting that property rights were not the divine right of kings or governments; they were natural rights derived from individual labor and effort. This placed the power of self-determination in every citizen's hands rather than the state's.

Locke's philosophy profoundly affected American independence and the formation of our republic. The Founding Fathers agreed that liberty was a hollow promise without property. Like Locke, they believed a government that failed to protect personal property was ineffective and illegitimate. Consequently, they designed a constitution with the primary purpose of safeguarding individual rights, including property.

"In what then does real power consist?" Noah Webster once asked. "The answer is short and plain—in property."[84] This simple declaration encapsulates the idea that self-determination and, by extension, ownership were critical to civic power in republican government.

James Madison's perspective on property was more nuanced than Webster's. Still, he believed protecting property rights—specifically how individuals acquire and

---

[83] John Locke, Two Treatises of Government, 1689.

[84] Noah Webster, A Citizen of America: An Examination Into the Leading Principles of America, October 17, 1787.

accumulate property—was vital to preserving personal freedom. "The diversity in the faculties of men, from which the rights of property originate, is not less an insuperable obstacle to a uniformity of interests. The protection of these faculties is the first object of government."[85]

These differences in faculties—talent, ambition, and circumstances—result in unequal outcomes. Madison realized this, considering them a requisite, even beneficial, aspect of a free society. Rather than alienating these faculties, the government's first objective is protecting them. "From the protection of different and unequal faculties of acquiring property, the possession of different degrees and kinds of property immediately results; and from the influence of these on the sentiments and views of the respective proprietors ensues a division of the society into different interests and parties."[86]

Madison knew these inequalities could fuel divisions and factions, creating competing societal interests. Yet he saw this diversity of views, interests, and ownership as a strength. It created a natural counterbalance to the consolidation of power, thus preventing any one group from dominating the others.

Even so, the Founders recognized the inherent dangers posed by the concentration of property. Noah Webster, for instance, stressed the importance of a "general and tolerably equal distribution of property," arguing that it was "the whole basis of national freedom."[87]

---

[85] James Madison, Federalist No. 10, November 22, 1787.

[86] James Madison, Federalist No. 10, November 22, 1787.

[87] Noah Webster, A Citizen of America: An Examination Into the Leading Principles of America, October 17, 1787.

John Adams reiterated Webster's thoughts, pointing to the relationship between property and power: "Harrington[88] has shewn that power always follows property. This I believe to be as infallible a maxim, in politicks, as, that action and re-action are equal, is in Mechanicks.[89] Nay I believe we may advance one step farther and affirm that the ballance of power in a society, accompanies the ballance of property in land . . . If the multitude is possessed of the ballance of real estate, the multitude will have the ballance of Power, and in that case the multitude will take care of the liberty, virtue, and interest of the multitude in all acts of government."[90]

As long as humans exist, so will inequality, power, and property. But, the Founding Fathers believed these forces were infinitely more bearable when held by the people at large rather than the state. This decentralization—not just of political but also of economic power—was at the heart of their vision for a free and just society.

While not as intensely focused on property rights as some of his predecessors, John Stuart Mill explored ownership's social and moral dimensions. He acknowledged property as a foundation for economic stability and personal freedom but was critical of wealth disparity. "It is some hardship to be born into the world and to find all nature's gifts previously engrossed, and no place left for the new-comer."[91]

Despite his advocacy for reform, Mill rejected the state's control of land and resources as advocated by socialism. He thought such systems would stifle individual liberty and

88 James Harrington, The Commonwealth of Oceania, 1656.

89 Isaac Newton, Mathematical Principles of Natural Philosophy, Third Law of Motion, 1687.

90 John Adams, Letter to James Sullivan, May 26, 1776.

91 John Stuart Mill, The Principles of Political Economy, 1848.

creativity. Nevertheless, his solution—state intervention—still presented opportunities for government overreach.

Lord John Dalberg-Acton, the 19th-century historian, perhaps best known for his maxim, "Power tends to corrupt, and absolute power corrupts absolutely,"[92] shared many of Mill's concerns about power and property but took his critique a step further by exploring the political dangers of concentrated economic control. Without property rights, Acton claimed the people would be left dependent on the state instead of themselves and, with this dependency, would lose their liberty.

In other words, true political freedom cannot exist without economic freedom, and property is the key to maintaining that balance. But to sustain a just republic, we have a moral obligation to accumulate property responsibly —just as we're bound to exercise our other freedoms without infringing on the rights of others.

St. Thomas Aquinas contended it was a matter of natural law to take possession of what was once common, but the possessor has a moral duty to ensure others aren't unfairly deprived. "A rich man does not act unlawfully if he anticipates someone in taking possession of something which at first was common property, and gives others a share: but he sins if he excludes others indiscriminately from using it."[93] This doesn't imply that the rich must give away their property. Instead, Aquinas called for generosity where the rich thrive and others languish.

Thinkers like Aquinas, Mill, Locke, and others all supported the idea of personal responsibility and moral obligation in property ownership. However, their belief in

____

92 Lord Acton, Letter to Bishop Mandell Creighton, April 5, 1887.
93 St. Thomas Aquinas, *Summa Theologica*, 1265-1274.

generosity must not be confused with charity enforced by the state's sword. Mill and especially Acton were highly skeptical of ideologies like socialism that sought to redistribute property through government intervention, seeing them as pathways to tyranny.

Ever watchful of centralized power, Thomas Jefferson was particularly wary of these ideologies. "To take from one, because it is thought that his own industry and that of his fathers has acquired too much, in order to spare to others, who, or whose fathers have not exercised equal industry and skill, is to violate arbitrarily the first principle of association, 'the guarantee to every one of a free exercise of his industry, and the fruits acquired by it.' If the overgrown wealth of an individual be deemed dangerous to the state, the best corrective is the law of equal inheritance to all in equal degree; and the better, as this enforces a law of nature, while extra-taxation violates it."[94]

Like many of his contemporaries, Jefferson understood the dangers of too much property in too few hands but disagreed with resolving the problem through excessive taxation or forced redistribution. Instead, he advocated reforms that applied equally to all—the foundation of his political philosophy in general.

Considering their stated positions on centralization, it follows that if the Founders intended power to rest with the people and if property is a primary power source, then modern America has undergone a troubling transformation. Today, property and, by extension, power are concentrated within a new aristocracy—corporations, political elites, and

---

[94] Thomas Jefferson, Letter to Joseph Milligan, Note Communicated to the Editor, April 16, 1816.

the supremely wealthy—mirroring the very concentration of power Locke spoke out against.

What, then, is the solution when the state itself works against the common man? Agricultural subsidies primarily benefit the largest farms, driving smaller competitors out of the market. Economic regulations more often stifle small businesses than protect the consumer—just as large corporations intend. Federal Reserve policy manipulates the financial markets, and the government has repeatedly implemented laws or policies that favor the aristocracy. Rather than reforming those laws, it blames the successful for the wealth disparity and seeks more power under the guise of equality.

Andrew Jackson's vehement opposition to the Second National Bank in 1832 offers a valuable parallel of the state working against the public interest. Jackson saw the Second National Bank as a monopoly that consolidated financial power and granted undue influence to the wealthy. "It is to be regretted that the rich and powerful too often bend the acts of government to their selfish purposes. Distinctions in society will always exist under every just government. Equality of talents, of education, or of wealth can not be produced by human institutions. In the full enjoyment of the gifts of Heaven and the fruits of superior industry, economy, and virtue, every man is equally entitled to protection by law; but when the laws undertake to add to these natural and just advantages artificial distinctions, to grant titles, gratuities, and exclusive privileges, to make the rich richer and the potent more powerful, the humble members of society-the farmers, mechanics, and laborers-who have neither the time nor the means of securing like favors to themselves, have a right to complain of the injustice of their Government."[95]

President Jackson's stance against monopoly reflects his broader opposition to any government action that created economic inequality or granted privileges to the elites at the common man's expense. As Jackson himself noted, "There are no necessary evils in government. Its evils exist only in its abuses. If it would confine itself to equal protection, and, as Heaven does its rains, shower its favors alike on the high and the low, the rich and the poor, it would be an unqualified blessing."[96]

While numerous reforms could provide equal opportunity and incentivize the decentralization of property, such measures will be meaningless if we fail to address the root of the corruption that plagues our republic. Let us not forget that Rome's republic fell to Caesar's ambition, but his fall did nothing to restore it since the corruption's source went unaddressed. Of what good was the Ides of March to the republic while Caesar's tyranny stood unscathed?

---

[95] Andrew Jackson, Veto Message Regarding the Bank of the United States, July 10, 1832.
[96] Andrew Jackson, Veto Message Regarding the Bank of the United States, July 10, 1832.

Economic Freedom

"It is characteristic of the unlearned that they are forever proposing something which is old, and, because it has recently come to their own attention, supposing it to be new." [97]

Calvin Coolidge

Since we are discussing property and wealth, it's only fitting to discuss the economy. The concept of the economy—how individuals relate to property and capital—is at the core of nearly all political discussions, particularly those concerning individual liberty.

Man must eat to survive. Just as indisputable a fact is that man must either provide for himself or rely on others for his provisions. While self-reliance carries risk, a man free to conduct business from his own estate, protected by his natural rights, is perfectly free. Economies emerge because most men lack the appetite or tolerance to depend solely upon themselves, preferring instead to exchange their labor for goods produced by others.

Many question why they should be forced to work merely to survive. Here, we return to the underlying truth: man must eat. If he's unwilling or unable to produce his own sustenance—seed the land and harvest the bounty himself— he must engage with others who are. Thus, a man enters the economy, seeking a more convenient or comfortable career, trading a portion of his labor for the farmer's production. This division of labor, where one might till the land while another forges the shovel, allows each individual to utilize

---

[97] Calvin Coolidge, Commencement Address at Holy Cross College, June 25, 1919.

the unique faculties best suited to them. Therein lies the elegance of a free economy.

Thomas Jefferson believed that an individual's ability to labor freely—since labor is an extension of personal autonomy—is essential to liberty. In his First Inaugural Address, he concisely articulated this philosophy. "A wise and frugal government, which shall restrain men from injuring one another, which shall leave them otherwise free to regulate their own pursuits of industry and improvement, and shall not take from the mouth of labor the bread it has earned. This is the sum of good government, and this is necessary to close the circle of our felicities."[98]

Although he addressed the inconsistent state legislatures of his time, James Madison unknowingly described our federal government's eventual condition. "It will be of little avail to the people, that the laws are made by men of their own choice, if the laws be so voluminous that they cannot be read, or so incoherent that they cannot be understood."[99]

Madison feared that such instability in lawmaking would lead to confusion, unpredictability, and corruption, benefiting the wealthy and politically savvy over the common man. "Every new regulation concerning commerce or revenue, or in any way affecting the value of the different species of property, presents a new harvest to those who watch the change and can trace its consequences; a harvest, reared not by themselves, but by the toils and cares of the great body of their fellow-citizens. This is a state of things in which it may be said with some truth that laws are made for the few, not for the many."[100]

---

[98] Thomas Jefferson, First Inaugural Address, March 4, 1801.

[99] James Madison, Federalist No. 62, February 27, 1788.

[100] James Madison, Federalist No. 62, February 27, 1788.

Thomas Jefferson had lived in France during the early days of their revolution, witnessed the U.S. Constitution in action, worked alongside George Washington, and clashed ideologically with Alexander Hamilton and John Adams. He saw the devastation wrought by the Napoleonic Wars, served two terms as President, presided over the Louisiana Purchase, signed the bill outlawing the transatlantic slave trade, and watched in horror as the British burned Washington D.C. during the War of 1812.

With this wealth of experience, Jefferson had become convinced of another looming threat to liberty: the national debt. "We must make our election between economy and liberty, or profusion and servitude," Jefferson advised. He foresaw a future where public debt could lead to oppressive taxation, stating that if debts continued to mount, Americans would be taxed in all aspects of life—"in our meat and in our drink, in our necessaries and our comforts, in our labors and our amusements, for our callings and our creeds."[101]

Ultimately, Jefferson predicted a dire outcome: "We shall come to labor sixteen hours in the twenty-four, give the earnings of fifteen of these to the government for their debts and daily expenses . . . have no time to think . . . and be glad to obtain subsistence by hiring ourselves to rivet chains on the necks of our fellow-sufferers."[102]

In the same letter, Jefferson elaborated that, much like personal recklessness can destroy private fortunes, public debt siphons away wealth through taxation and government intervention. Once the government sets such a precedent, straying from its founding principles, society becomes passive, apathetic, and powerless. "Mere automatons of

---

[101] Thomas Jefferson, Letter to Samuel Kerchival, July 12, 1816.
[102] Thomas Jefferson, Letter to Samuel Kerchival, July 12, 1816.

misery, to have no sensibilities left but for sinning and suffering. Then begins, indeed, the *bellum omnium in omnia* [103] . . . Taxation follows that, and in its train wretchedness and oppression."[104]

The national debt now stands at over $30 trillion, with each taxpayer shouldering their share. Americans find themselves increasingly reliant on a government that, far from protecting their liberties, demands more of their labor and earnings. Jefferson's prediction that people might labor sixteen hours daily to make ends meet under a corrupt government becomes a familiar and prescient concern.

The government's reliance on debt has shifted the focus away from fostering free markets and competition. The laws and regulations governing commerce and revenue are now so voluminous and incoherent that only those with the resources to navigate or manipulate the system genuinely benefit. Corporations with the means to lobby Congress thrive, while smaller businesses and individuals struggle to keep up. This is the modern-day equivalent of Madison's "harvest reared not by themselves, but by the toils and cares of the great body of their fellow-citizens."

The COVID-19 pandemic provided a notable example of economic interference. The government defined "essential" business, which favored large corporations and forced many small businesses to shut their doors permanently. In other words, the government handpicked the winners and losers. Meanwhile, trillions of dollars in relief funds were sent out in a lopsided distribution, and the resulting inflation, far from

---

[103] Thomas Hobbes, Leviathan, Translates to "the war of all against all," 1651.

[104] Thomas Jefferson, Letter to Samuel Kerchival, July 12, 1816.

"transitory,"[105] became a hidden tax that still hurts most Americans to this day.

Beyond the debt itself, America's tax structure desperately needs repair. While the stated goal of progressive taxation is to reduce inequality, the wealthy more easily navigate the complex tax codes, often leaving the middle class to bear the burden.[106]

So here we are, staring at an economy shaped by corruption and manipulation, with a population overburdened by taxation and oppression while corporations grow wealthier. As evidenced by the warnings of Jefferson, Madison, Webster, and many other Founding Fathers, this economy was never their intention. It's the inevitable result of a powerful central government trampling on public liberty and enriching the aristocracy.

With all these concerns—the overwhelming national debt, favoritism toward large corporations, and unequal opportunities—many Americans have understandably lost faith in the system. They see our economy as the result of too much liberty rather than too little. This disillusionment has led to growing calls for sweeping changes, from increased government control to outright socialism or even communism.

The appeal is clear: if the current system seems rigged, wouldn't a more equal distribution of wealth fix these problems? Wouldn't a more centralized government be able to correct inequality and ensure a fairer playing field for all?

As the socialist Oscar Wilde observed, "The emotions of man are stirred more quickly than man's intelligence,"[107]

---

[105] Janet Yellen, Treasury Secretary, Press Conference, May 2021.
[106] Tax Policy Center, Distributional Analysis of Tax Proposals, 2019.
[107] Oscar Wilde, The Soul of Man Under Socialism, 1891.

which is why emotionally driven "solutions" overlook the problem's source by design. If the state has enabled corruption and manipulation, failing at its core duties within a free market, why would it suddenly improve once given complete control over our health, wealth, and livelihoods?

Furthermore, what kind of equality do we truly desire? Our nation was founded on the principle of equality under the law, which ensures that the government treats all citizens equally, regardless of their status. Closely aligned with this concept is equality of opportunity, another cornerstone of American philosophy, which provides everyone a fair chance to succeed based on their abilities and efforts.

On the other hand, there are certain aspects of life—talents, intelligence, resourcefulness, physical features, and circumstances—where equality might be desirable in some respects but delusional in reality. Then, there's equality of outcome or the idea that everyone should "end up in the same place," regardless of individual effort or merit. Karl Marx expressed this ideology in communism as, "From each according to his ability, to each according to his needs."[108]

Philosophers have pondered this question for millennia, and we must also ask it: what is justice? Do we believe a just government is one in which the state treats everyone equally under the law, regardless of race, religion, or gender? Shouldn't politicians be held to the same legal standards as assembly line workers? Shouldn't the wealthy face imprisonment for the same offenses as the poor? Shouldn't a woman be able to speak her mind with the same rights as a man? If we value this equality, we must recognize it

---

[108] Karl Marx, Critique of the Gotha Program, 1875.

invariably leads to some achieving more than others based on their skills, efforts, and decisions.

However, suppose we prioritize material equality above all else, as socialism, communism, and other collectivist economies do. In that case, the law must necessarily treat individuals unequally, favoring some over others—one man over another. Isn't this the complaint many have about our current system? Is this not the very definition of oppression? Is this not injustice?

The 20th-century economist Friedrich Hayek articulated the point well. "Equality before the law and material equality are therefore not only different but are in conflict with each other; and we can achieve either the one or the other, but not both at the same time."[109]

Without the security property rights offer, man must speak and act to ensure his continued survival under the all-powerful state's rule. If he cannot dissent without fear of losing his livelihood, where, then, is his freedom of speech? And if he has forfeited his right to bear arms, how should he ever regain his rights?

Yes, we should return the American system to one of equal opportunity under the law. Yes, there should be a more equal distribution of property, and yes, the wealthy have a moral responsibility to aid those less fortunate, but force is not charity; it's tyranny.

---

[109] Friedrich Hayek, The Constitution of Liberty, 1960.

Socialism

"The belief, not only of the socialists but also of those so-called liberals who are diligently preparing the way for them, is that by due skill an ill-working humanity may be framed into well-working institutions. It is a delusion. The defective natures of citizens will show themselves in the bad acting of whatever social structure they are arranged into. There is no political alchemy by which you can get golden conduct out of leaden instincts." [110]

Herbert Spencer

The United States was founded on a revolutionary principle: the government exists only to protect natural rights, ensuring liberty and equality under the law. Private property and the right to acquire it is a pillar of this philosophy, offering the satisfaction of enjoying the fruits of one's labor and protection from tyranny. The prominent French economist Jean-Baptiste Say described this idea of individual liberty as the engine of prosperity. "Who will attempt to deny, that the certainty of enjoying the fruits of one's land, capital, and labor is the most powerful inducement to render them productive?"[111]

Where free markets rely on individual effort and personal incentives, socialism demands a different approach, exchanging liberty and equal opportunity for the promise of material equality. Their ideals are noble—ending hunger and homelessness and reducing wealth disparity—but their proposed methods significantly threaten personal freedom. No matter the particular species, from democratic socialism

---

[110] Herbert Spencer, Man Versus the State, 1884.

[111] Jean-Baptiste Say, A Treatise on Political Economy, 1803.

to communism, socialists advocate for varying degrees of centralized control, communal ownership of business, and wealth redistribution.

As a nation born from an unquenchable thirst for liberty, forcibly redistributing property contradicts the reason for our government's existence and perverts the moral principle of equal treatment. Jean-Baptiste Say, warning of central control, put it succinctly. "It would be a gross violation of the right of property, to saddle one class of society with the compulsory maintenance of another; and it would be a violation still more gross, to give one set of men a personal control over another; for the freedom of personal action is the most sacred of all the objects of property."[112]

Yet socialism persists. Why? One explanation could lie in its ambiguity. The 19th-century British Prime Minister Lord Salisbury pointed out, "Where they are agreed, they are not precise; and where they are precise, they are not agreed."[113] This lack of precision allows socialists to rally around lofty ideals and appeal to emotion over reason—all while absolving themselves of socialism's past failures.

From Lenin and Stalin's Soviet Union to Maoist China, Cuba to North Korea, Venezuela, East Germany, Yugoslavia, India, and others, the disastrous results of socialist and communist regimes in the last century are well-documented, and whatever short-term successes they may have experienced are almost exclusively due to the United States subsidizing their efforts through economic, military, humanitarian, or financial aid.

That said, few realize the United States itself was the proving ground for over 200 socialist experiments in the

[112] Jean-Baptiste Say, A Treatise on Political Economy, 1803.

[113] Robert Arthur Talbot Gascoyne-Cecil, Speech on Socialism, May 24, 1890.

19th century. These small-scale projects failed just as spectacularly, offering us a preview of socialism's inevitable outcomes, regardless of scope.

Ranging from a hundred to a few thousand members, groups like the North American Phalanx, Brook Farm, and New Harmony sprang up across America, aiming to build fair societies based on shared labor and common ownership. Despite denominational differences, these communities shared three defining characteristics: membership was selective, life inside was tightly regulated, and devotion to the commune was paramount.

At first, the energy was palpable. Visitors flocked to these communities, eager to witness a living experiment in equality. But one after another, excitement evaporated when a commune encountered hardship. Even with a shared purpose, crop failures, food shortages, or financial instability ended many communes within a year and most others within five.

Why? Top-down control makes a man no more happy in the long term than top-down economics makes him wealthy. Class structures didn't vanish; they reorganized. Factions emerged, and power struggles erupted when leadership changed. In equal wage systems, outdoor workers envied those with lighter indoor duties. In variable wage systems, those inside felt shortchanged by the outdoor laborer's higher pay. To seek remedy, people's only means of protesting was skipping work, which could be met with deprivation or exile. The 20th-century mass casualties proved what eventually happens under socialism when participation is mandatory, and exile isn't an option.

Contrary to socialist theory, men found other means to exploit one another without private property. Some communes fell to fraud and corruption, while others crumbled because of favoritism and labor collusion. In the end, some members felt laziness was rewarded over dedication to the collective, driving away the skilled workers needed to maintain the community and its productivity.[114]

The greatest casualty of these communes, however, might have been the human spirit. While perpetually teetering on the brink of starvation or insolvency, strict regulations left little time or energy for personal expression, creativity, or the arts. Education was designed to create obedient workers, and children were raised as tools to fulfill specific needs. As socialism's opponents have often argued, "This whole created being—man—is reduced to matter."[115]

Under ideal conditions—hand-picking their members, land, and industries—these communities all failed, offering a lesson: the truths of human nature and economics can't be wished away merely because they're inconvenient.

Regardless of their repeated failures, socialistic ideas continue to seduce those disillusioned with reality's inequalities. One of history's greatest philosophers on human nature, Aristotle, highlighted a deeper philosophical problem with the pursuit of equality. "It is not the possessions but the desires of mankind which require to be equalized, and this is impossible."[116] While he theorized that education and governance could help mold desires toward a common good, he would have been wary of the extreme control needed to implement such a system on a large scale.

This extent of control is the antithesis of a free society under political democracy. In a free society, man has the

---

[114] Morris Hillquit, History of Socialism in the United States, 1903.
[115] Aleksandr Solzhenitsyn, Washington D.C. Speech, July 9, 1975.
[116] Aristotle, Politics, Book II, 325-323 BC.

right and economic liberty to determine his worth—whether by pursuing wealth, advocating for social change, or simply living a life of personal fulfillment. This journey is the tangible expression of free thought. Yet, the socialist's quest for equity requires one man to become privileged at the systemic devaluation of another's talents and abilities. By assigning an arbitrary value to man's contributions, socialism robs him of property and the basic human dignity he's fought tyrants throughout history to secure. Is this discriminatory exercise of force not the very definition of tyranny?[117]

At the same time, socialism is promoted as a system where the people are in charge, collectively controlling production—a concept referred to as "economic democracy." However, socialism isn't strictly an economic system; it requires extensive authority and demands drastic political changes to enforce conformity and suppress dissent from those unwilling to participate. In effect, by consolidating the political power needed to impose economic democracy, socialism destroys political democracy. Indeed, this new form of democracy shares more in common with a family vote: it gives the illusion of choice until the majority clashes with the interests of those actually in control.

Alexis de Tocqueville, the French historian best known for *Democracy in America*, recognized this incompatibility over 150 years ago. "Democracy and socialism are not interdependent concepts," he said in a brilliant speech. "They are not only different, but opposing philosophies. Democracy extends the sphere of personal independence; socialism confines it. Democracy values each man at his highest;

---

[117] Tyranny: arbitrary or despotic exercise of power, Noah Webster's American Dictionary of the English Language, 1828.

socialism makes of each man an agent, an instrument, a number. Democracy and socialism have but one thing in common—equality. But note well the difference. Democracy aims at equality in liberty. Socialism desires equality in constraint and in servitude."[118]

If socialism excels at anything, it's in being incompatible with democracy and human nature itself. Where freedom tolerates socialism, socialism cannot tolerate freedom. When freedom leads to unequal outcomes, socialists blame extreme wealth for society's ills rather than the wickedness of man. In response, they prescribe equal materialism, trading freedom for control, and believe man's desire for wealth and power will vanish once his basic needs are met. Moreover, by claiming man is shaped solely by his conditions, socialists effectively deny free will exists and reduce him to something mechanical without the capacity for autonomy.

One doesn't need to look any further than prison—where equality of provisions, housing, and activities are strictly enforced—to see how quickly this assumption falls apart. It's not the labor or equality prisoners despise; it's the force that creates this "equality." Searching for any way to reclaim their humanity or experience some form of independence, inmates are renowned for their ingenuity in finding ways to exploit, circumvent, and resist their environment, even when every material need is met.

While socialism might offer some the "equality" they think they desire, it chokes the human spirit, becoming an emotional and intellectual prison for others. And where is justice when free men are imprisoned simply because others enjoy the "security" of life behind bars?

---

[118] Alexis de Tocqueville, Speech on Socialism at Constituent Assembly, 1848.

Fyodor Dostoevsky was a nobleman in 19th-century Russia who sympathized with utopian socialism. At 28 years old, he was arrested and sentenced to death for his involvement with a group advocating social change. However, moments before his scheduled execution, Tsar Nicholas I commuted Dostoevsky's sentence to four years of hard labor in Siberia. This experience, alongside his spiritual awakening, transformed the Russian novelist into a staunch opponent of socialism. He believed socialism ignored the complexities of human nature—particularly man's capacity for irrationality—and was inherently immoral. "You say, science itself will teach man (though to my mind it's a superfluous luxury) that he never has really had any caprice or will of his own, and that he himself is something of the nature of a piano-key . . . Even if man really were nothing but a piano-key, even if this were proved to him by natural science and mathematics, even then he would not become reasonable, but would purposely do something perverse out of simple ingratitude . . . the whole work of man really seems to consist in nothing but proving to himself every minute that he is a man and not a piano-key!"[119]

Socialists don't propose man will work less, nor do they offer him more leisure time. They don't even suggest he'll enjoy a better job. In fact, under socialism's ceiling, man will still labor to survive—but as a piano key. And if a man were content merely to labor and survive, he would have long settled for caves as homes and monarchs for rulers. Instead, he has endured centuries of bloodshed in pursuit of liberty and self-governance. No, chains are not a necessary evil, and freedom is never born from its own destruction. The only

---

[119] Fyodor Dostoevsky, Notes from the Underground, 1864.

thing socialism guarantees is perhaps its most damning contradiction: it wishes to "cure" man's selfishness, corruption, and greed by enslaving him to a system ruled by the selfish, the corrupt, and the greedy.

The Majority

"If ever the free institutions of America are destroyed, that event may be attributed to the unlimited authority of the majority, which may at some future time urge the minorities to desperation, and oblige them to have recourse to physical force. Anarchy will then be the result, but it will have been brought about by despotism." [120]

Alexis de Tocqueville

The will of the majority is, without question, the foundation of democratic governance and a necessary component of the American political system. In a perfect world, the majority would be guided by a solid ethical foundation, serving as society's collective conscience. It would value justice and equality above all else, never benefitting one group while trampling on another's rights, liberty, or dignity. But history has shown us that this utopian vision of majority rule has seldom been realized for long.

In reality, the will of the many is not always the will of the good, and the majority's power must be balanced by some other means. Neither truth nor righteousness can be determined by vote, and justice can't be harvested from the seeds of injustice, no matter how many support it. The majority can only decide what is tolerable *to them* at any given moment. And when their will is driven by passion instead of reason or self-interest over justice, the results can be catastrophic.

As John Stuart Mill cautioned, this unchecked majority rule isn't infallible and can quickly devolve into social

---

[120] Alexis de Tocqueville, Democracy in America, 1835.

tyranny. "The people, consequently, may desire to oppress a part of their number; and precautions are as much needed against this as against any other abuse of power."[121]

Reinhold Niebuhr, a renowned American theologian and ethicist, observed that individuals often surrender personal responsibility when acting as part of a group, delegating their moral accountability to the collective. He wrote that men find solace in larger groups and believe themselves ethical because they're part of a majority. When people act in groups, their sense of responsibility falters, allowing them to tolerate or even endorse actions they would find indefensible as individuals. Thus, when the majority abdicates individual conscience, the moral fabric of society begins to fray.[122]

Our most sincere hope is that truth, "tolerability," and righteousness all align with the majority's will. At best, history paints an unflattering portrait of majority rule. The ancient city-state of Athens—the cradle of democracy—provides one of the earliest examples. The Athenian assembly, driven by emotion rather than wisdom, made disastrous decisions, most notably the ill-fated Sicilian Expedition[123] during the Peloponnesian War. This decision, motivated by popular sentiment instead of reasoned strategy, crippled Athens and contributed to its eventual downfall.

Reflecting on the volatility of such majorities, James Madison wrote that even the greatest minds can't prevent a

---

[121] John Stuart Mill, On Liberty, 1859.

[122] Reinhold Niebuhr, Moral Man and Immoral Society, 1932.

[123] The Sicilian Expedition (415–413 BC) was a disastrous Athenian military campaign during the Peloponnesian War, aimed at conquering Syracuse in Sicily. Despite initial optimism, the expedition faltered due to poor leadership, internal division, and strong resistance from Syracuse, aided by Sparta. The defeat crippled Athens' military strength, with the loss of nearly the entire fleet and army, and significantly weakened Athens' position in the Peloponnesian War. This failure contributed to Athens' eventual downfall, marking a turning point toward its defeat by Sparta in 404 BC.

mob's self-destruction. "Passion never fails to wrest the sceptre from reason. Had every Athenian citizen been a Socrates, every Athenian assembly would still have been a mob."[124]

Rome, too, was a victim of majoritarian rule. Despite its elaborate system of checks and balances, the Roman Republic began to fracture as Julius Caesar manipulated the assemblies and masses, leading to the Republic's collapse. Cicero, witnessing Rome's fall in real time, warned: "A multitude of men may be just as tyrannical as a single despot; and it is so much the worse since no monster can be more barbarous than the mob, which assumes the name and appearance of the people."[125] The mob, swayed by Caesar's promises of wealth and power, eventually dismantled the very republic it intended to protect.

The French Revolution is another sobering example of democracy descending into chaos. British philosopher Edmund Burke criticized France's embrace of radical democracy, forewarning, "In a democracy the majority of the citizens is capable of exercising the most cruel oppressions upon the minority . . . and will be carried on with much greater fury, than can almost ever be apprehended from the dominion of a single sceptre."[126]

What began as a movement for liberty and equality soon spiraled into the Reign of Terror. The Jacobins, claiming to represent the people's will, turned to the guillotine and carried out mass executions in the name of justice. The Revolution ultimately devoured itself and paved the way for

---

[124] James Madison, Federalist No. 55, February 15, 1788.

[125] Cicero, On the Commonwealth, 54-51BC.

[126] Edmund Burke, Reflections on the Revolution in France, 1790.

Napoleon's rise to power—a man who would, in the name of empire, bring death to millions across Europe.

The Weimar Republic in Germany provides a 20th-century parallel of democratic failures. Hyperinflation, political extremism, and economic instability allowed Adolf Hitler to gain power through democratic elections. He then swiftly dismantled democracy and installed himself as dictator. Such men are rarely secretive about their plans, and Hitler was no exception. For years before his election, the future dictator was open about his disdain for democracy, parliamentary government, and the rule of law.[127] Yet the Germans didn't listen and elected the despot, completely dismissing the obvious warning signs.

Decades earlier, Herbert Spencer asked, "If people by a plebiscite elect a man despot over them, do they remain free because the despotism was of their own making?"[128] Along that same line, since Hitler used democratic means and the majority's support to seize power, did that make his tyranny more tolerable or his genocide less evil?

Venezuela is a contemporary example of democracy transforming into authoritarianism. Elected in 1998 on promises of popular democracy, economic reform, and social justice, Hugo Chávez introduced constitutional changes that concentrated power in the executive. Over the next fifteen years, Chávez's socialist policies weakened the democratic safeguards that once checked government authority. His successor, Nicolás Maduro, deepened the authoritarian grip, using fraudulent elections and state force to maintain power. The result is a failed economy, rampant inflation, and widespread food and medicine shortages.

---

[127] Adolf Hitler, Mein Kampf, 1926.

[128] Herbert Spencer, Man Versus State, 1884.

Indeed, as John Adams wrote, "Democracy never lasts long. It soon wastes, exhausts, and murders itself."[129] James Madison was equally well-versed in democracy's history and said, "Such democracies have ever been spectacles of turbulence and contention; have ever been found incompatible with personal security, or the rights of property; and have, in general, been as short in their lives as they have been violent in their deaths."[130]

The previous and many other examples illustrate a fundamental truth: the majority cannot check its own power. When driven by an agenda, ideology, or impulsive behavior, men make foolish decisions that can harm others or even themselves. In large numbers, these same men don't suddenly become rational simply because they've been corralled into a singular voting bloc. No, the majority doesn't explicitly vote for dictatorship, famine, or genocide, but these outcomes emerge when chaos, expedience, or self-interest trump reason.

As Madison wisely remarked, "No man is allowed to be a judge in his own cause; because his interest would certainly bias his judgment, and, not improbably, corrupt his integrity. With equal, nay, with greater reason, a body of men are unfit to be both judges and parties."[131]

When the majority chooses its own leaders and policies, it validates its own authority. At the same time, it tacitly submits to the methods used to achieve its goals. This cycle—where the majority rules, then rules because it's the majority—continues even when those methods oppress the minority,

---

[129] John Adams, Letter to John Taylor, 1814.
[130] James Madison, Federalist No. 10, November 22, 1787.
[131] James Madison, Federalist No. 10, November 22, 1787.

who, lacking in power and representation, has no peaceable recourse.

A need shared by a million people is still just one need, which is countered by the single, equal need of one. And if the majority can't be pleased without sacrificing the equal rights and needs of the one, how can their decision be righteous? At the cost of one person, a majority's moral superiority crumbles. Would a majority, perfectly willing to alienate one man, stop at the alienation of ten or ten million?

This is why we demand more from a majority than simply greater numbers. Without higher principles like justice, equality under the law, or even consideration of the minority itself, a majority risks becoming nothing more than a mob. "What we here seek," Herbert Spencer wrote, "is some higher warrant for the subordination of minority to majority than that arising from inability to resist physical coercion."[132]

The Founding Fathers knew well the danger of centralized power—whether in the hands of a single despot or a multitude of them—and designed a republican system that incorporated democratic elements to prevent unchecked power. The House of Representatives channels the majority's will. Formerly chosen by republican means, the Senate is supposed to check that will, and the president checks both legislative branches.

However, the Senate is now selected by popular vote,[133] and the Electoral College—originally a hybrid of democratic and republican methods—has steadily become more democratized. While the Electoral College still provides smaller states with proportionally more influence in the President's election, its electors are bound to their state's

---

[132] Herbert Spencer, Man Versus the State, 1884.

[133] The 17th Amendment established the direct election of senators. 1913.

popular vote in most cases. This general shift toward pure democracy in the legislative and executive branches undermines the republican safeguards meant to protect us from the democratic failures of Athens and Rome.

If the Electoral College were abolished, minority interests would not be represented at a federal level. Political power would, therefore, concentrate in America's largest urban centers, leaving rural areas marginalized, their voices drowned by the tides of "progress."[134] Combined with the wealth disparity and the rise of America's aristocracy, the conditions would resemble those that ultimately led to the French Revolution. In light of history, that possibility should terrify us all.

"It is of great importance in a republic," James Madison wrote in *Federalist No. 51*, "not only to guard the society against the oppression of its rulers, but to guard one part of the society against the injustice of the other part. Different interests necessarily exist in different classes of citizens. If a majority be united by a common interest, the rights of the minority will be insecure."[135] The Father of the Constitution was acutely aware of how public sentiment can change with the winds—or even be manipulated. "A common passion or interest will, in almost every case, be felt by a majority of the whole; a communication and concert, results from the form of government itself; and there is nothing to check the

---

[134] At approximately 40 million people, California is more populated than Connecticut, Utah, Iowa, Nevada, Arkansas, Kansas, Mississippi, New Mexico, Nebraska, Idaho, West Virginia, Hawaii, New Hampshire, Maine, Montana, Rhode Island, Delaware, South Dakota, North Dakota, Alaska, Vermont, and Wyoming combined. At four million people, Los Angeles itself is more populated than any one of these 22 states.

[135] James Madison, Federalist No. 51, February 6, 1788.

inducements to sacrifice the weaker party, or an obnoxious individual."[136]

Alexander Hamilton also advised against pure democracy. "It has been observed by an honorable gentleman, that a pure democracy, if it were practicable, would be the most perfect government. Experience has proved, that no position in politics is more false than this. The ancient democracies, in which the people themselves deliberated, never possessed one feature of good government. Their very character was tyranny; their figure deformity."[137]

Thomas Jefferson, often cited in favor of majority rule, carefully qualified his support. "The majority is in all cases to prevail. But that will, to be rightful, must be reasonable; that the minority possess their equal rights, which equal laws must protect, and to violate which would be oppression."[138]

And oppression is what we wish to avoid, isn't it? There is no greater danger to liberty than a majority that has lost its moral bearings, though convinced its judgment remains sound. Yes, the majority determines what it will tolerate, but the minority can keep society tethered to what's right. Where the majority follows the path of least resistance, the minority endures humiliation and persecution for the sake of righteousness. It seems to be in this tension between righteousness and tolerability that the fate of every society is determined.

For true freedom and real progress, the majority should ask: "What is good, and does that good impact everyone equally?" If it doesn't, then it is oppression because the

---

[136] James Madison, Federalist No. 10, November 22, 1787.

[137] Alexander Hamilton, First Speech at New York Ratifying Convention, June 21, 1788.

[138] Thomas Jefferson, Inaugural Address, 1801.

majority represents concentrated authority within one group. This centralization, whether political, societal, or economic, is the root of tyranny and injustice—the common thread throughout this work. In contrast, where power is distributed, there is liberty, and the free man, acting with agency and accountability, becomes the greatest protector of that liberty.

An Imperfect System

"The basis of our political systems is the right of the people to make and to alter their Constitutions of Government. But the Constitution which at any time exists, till changed by an explicit and authentic act of the whole people, is sacredly obligatory upon all." [139]

George Washington

Throughout this work, I've emphasized the dangers of centralized power and the corresponding erosion of individual rights. Some may misinterpret this critique as a monolithic defense of the original Constitution, dismissing the changes since its ratification. On the contrary, the Constitution was—and still is—imperfect. But it serves as the framework through which we can achieve greater liberty.

The Founding Fathers themselves had no illusions of crafting a flawless document. They understood that each state's varying interests demanded compromise for the sake of union. In a speech, Benjamin Franklin said, "I agree to this Constitution, with all its faults."[140]

Similarly, George Washington wrote to the esteemed Marquis de Lafayette, "Nor am I yet such an enthusiastic, partial or undiscriminating admirer of [the Constitution], as not to perceive it is tinctured with some real (though not radical) defects."[141]

Alexander Hamilton conceded, "I never expect to see a perfect work from imperfect man," and James Madison

---

[139] George Washington, Farewell Address, September 19, 1796.

[140] Benjamin Franklin, Speech at the Constitutional Convention, September 17, 1787.

[141] George Washington, Letter to Marquis de Lafayette, February 7, 1788.

acknowledged, "It has never been denied, by the friends of [the Constitution] on the table, that it has defects; but they do not think that it contains any real danger."[142]

However, a deeper criticism gained popularity in the 1800s: that by permitting slavery and failing to guarantee equal rights, the assertion "all men are created equal"[143] was never intended to include "all." Critics then, as they do now, argued the Constitution was written to protect only the interests of white, landowning men.

Through a modern lens, it isn't easy to reconcile the Founders' principles of liberty with the reality that some of them owned human beings. This contradiction wasn't lost on them. John Adams, for example, refused to own slaves. "Every measure of prudence, therefore, ought to be assumed for the eventual total extirpation of slavery from the United States."[144]

George Mason, a staunch critic of federal overreach, also refused to sign the Constitution, in large part because it failed to take more decisive action against slavery. Gouverneur Morris, who authored much of the Constitution's final language, was outspoken in his condemnation of the institution, famously asking, "Are they men? Then make them citizens and let them vote."[145]

Likewise, James Madison didn't shy away from addressing slavery in the United States. "We have seen the mere distinction of colour made in the most enlightened period of time, a ground of the most oppressive dominion ever exercised by man over man. What has been the source

---

[142] James Madison, Speech at the Virginia Ratifying Convention, June 6, 1788.

[143] Thomas Jefferson, The Declaration of Independence, July 4, 1776.

[144] John Adams, Letter to Robert J. Evans, June 8, 1819.

[145] Gouverneur Morris, James Madison's Notes on the Federal Convention, August 8, 1787.

of those unjust laws complained of among ourselves? Has it not been the real or supposed interest of the major number?"[146]

At the time of his death, George Washington was one of the wealthiest men in America. In his will, he provided for the emancipation of his slaves upon his wife's death. This was no simple gesture, as under Virginia law, freeing slaves was both a complex and expensive process.

Jefferson was many things, but he wasn't a savvy businessman like Washington. By his death, Jefferson was deeply in debt, and his estate, including his slaves, had to be sold to settle his creditors. Though he could not make the same gesture as Washington, Jefferson spent much of his life grappling with slavery and working to end it. "The abolition of domestic slavery is the great object of desire in those colonies, where it was unhappily introduced in their infant state . . . our repeated attempts to effect this by prohibitions, and by imposing duties which might amount to a prohibition, have been hitherto defeated."[147]

In the original draft of the Declaration of Independence, Jefferson condemned the transatlantic slave trade, accusing King George III of waging a "cruel war against human nature itself."[148] As a member of the Virginia House of Burgesses, Jefferson proposed laws for the gradual emancipation of slaves and sought to prohibit their further importation into Virginia. Later, as a member of the Continental Congress, he proposed the Ordinance of 1784, which would have banned slavery in all new western territories after 1800. And though

---

[146] James Madison, Notes on the Federal Convention, June 6, 1787.

[147] Thomas Jefferson, A Summary View of the Rights of British America, 1774.

[148] Thomas Jefferson, First Draft, The Declaration of Independence, 1776.

he wasn't directly involved in the final draft of the Northwest Ordinance,[149] it was based on his earlier proposals.

In 1785, Jefferson's *Notes on the State of Virginia* revealed his grave concerns about slavery's corrosive effects on society. "The whole commerce between master and slave is a perpetual exercise of the most boisterous passions, the most unremitting despotism on the one part, and degrading submissions on the other. Our children see this, and learn to imitate it."[150]

By then, abolitionist sentiments were rapidly growing in the North. Jefferson even predicted, "In a few years there will be no slaves northward of Maryland."[151] Ratifying the Constitution three years later, perhaps Jefferson and the other Founders hoped the winds of abolition would continue to strengthen and that an authentic act of the people would finally put an end to the abomination.

As president, Jefferson signed the Act Prohibiting the Importation of Slaves, taking a significant legal step toward curbing the institution. However, his most direct denunciation of slavery might have come in an 1814 letter to Thomas Cooper, in which he distinguished the moral contrast between the United States and Great Britain. "Do not mistake me. I am not advocating slavery. I am not justifying the wrongs we have committed on a foreign people, by the example of another nation committing equal wrongs on their own subjects. On the contrary, there is nothing I would not sacrifice to a practicable plan of

---

[149] The Northwest Ordinance: Chartered a government for the Northwest Territory, installing a system for the admission of new states and the prohibition of slavery in new territories. 1787.

[150] Thomas Jefferson, Notes on the State of Virginia, 1785.

[151] Thomas Jefferson, Letter to Dr. Price, August 7, 1785.

abolishing every vestige of this moral and political depravity."[152]

All this to say, the Founding Fathers clearly recognized slavery as a moral stain on the body and soul of America. Still, they struggled with simultaneously preserving the union, averting economic collapse, and balancing all rights.

Despite their inability or unwillingness to do more, Abraham Lincoln argued that the Constitution had placed slavery on the course of ultimate extinction. He pointed to the Northwest Ordinance and other congressional acts as evidence that the Founders intended to rid the nation of the peculiar institution. "The plain unmistakable spirit of that age, towards slavery, was hostility to the principle, and toleration, only by necessity."[153]

Even Alexander Stephens, Vice President of the Confederacy, who is rightfully criticized for his infamous *Cornerstone Speech*, admitted the Founders sought equality for all—Stephens simply believed they were wrong to do so. "The prevailing ideas entertained by [Jefferson] and most of the leading statesmen at the time of the formation of the old constitution, were that the enslavement of the African was in violation of the laws of nature; that it was wrong in principle, socially, morally, and politically. It was an evil they knew not well how to deal with, but the general opinion of the men of that day was that, somehow or other in the order of Providence, the institution would be evanescent and pass away. This idea, though not incorporated in the constitution, was the prevailing idea at that time . . . Those ideas, however, were fundamentally wrong."[154]

---

[152] Thomas Jefferson, Letter to Thomas Cooper, September 10, 1814.

[153] Abraham Lincoln, Peoria Speech, October 16, 1854.

[154] Alexander Stephens, Cornerstone Speech, March 21, 1861.

Frederick Douglass, who famously escaped the brutalities of slavery, once believed—as some do today—that the Constitution was inherently a racist, pro-slavery document. Reflecting on his early years, he remarked, "When I escaped from slavery, and was introduced to the Garrisonians,[155] I adopted very many of their opinions, and defended them just as long as I deemed them true. I was young, had read but little, and naturally took some things on trust."[156]

However, through careful study of the Constitution, Douglass began to challenge his earlier views, wondering how the Constitution could be pro-slavery if it didn't contain the term itself. He concluded this was no mere oversight but a deliberate omission by the framers. "If the Constitution were intended to be, by its framers and adopters, a slave-holding instrument, why neither 'slavery,' 'slaveholding,' nor 'slave' can anywhere be found in it?"[157]

A masterful orator, Frederick Douglass used metaphor to explain his determination. "The American Government and the American Constitution are spoken of in a manner which would naturally lead the hearer to believe that one is identical with the other; when the truth is, they are distinct in character as is a ship and a compass. The one may point right and the other steer wrong."[158] He then added a simple yet powerful observation. "[The Constitution's] language is 'we the people;' not we the white people, not even we the citizens, not we the privileged class, not we the high . . . but we the people, we the human inhabitants; and, if Negroes are

---

[155] Garrisonians: Radical abolitionists led by William Lloyd Garrison who believed the U.S. Constitution was a pro-slavery document and advocated for immediate abolition, even if it meant dissolving the Union.

[156] Frederick Douglass, Speech in Glasgow, Scotland, March 26, 1860.

[157] Frederick Douglass, What to the Slave is the Forth of July?, July 5, 1852.

[158] Frederick Douglass, Speech in Glasgow, Scotland, March 26, 1860.

people, they are included in the benefits for which the Constitution of America was ordained and established."[159]

Although we overlook the act's significance today, Mr. Douglass greatly respected our Founders' steps to end the transatlantic slave trade. "Men, at that time, both in England and in America, looked upon the slave trade as the life of slavery. The abolition of the slave trade was supposed to be the certain death of slavery. Cut off the stream, and the pond will dry up."[160]

Ultimately, Douglass argued that, when rightly applied, the Constitution could lead every person toward greater justice and equality. "Interpreted as it ought to be interpreted, the Constitution is a glorious liberty document."[161]

Even though the American government had its failings, the Constitution succeeded in providing the framework for abolishing slavery and extending civil rights to all. These examples show how change should be approached: universal principles focusing on expanding liberty without trampling minority rights or undermining the safeguards against tyranny. Righteous reform respects the balance of freedom and restraint, rejecting the allure of centralized power as a shortcut to progress.

History reminds us that while empires rise and fall, their ideals, philosophies, and arts—those human expressions of inherent value—persevere throughout the ages. President Coolidge said, "The Phoenician galleys and the civilization which was born of their commerce have perished, but the alphabet which that people perfected remains. The shepherd

---

[159] Frederick Douglass, Speech in Glasgow, Scotland, March 26, 1860.

[160] Frederick Douglass, Speech in Glasgow, Scotland, March 26, 1860.

[161] Frederick Douglass, What to the Slave is the Forth of July?, July 5, 1852.

kings of Israel, the temple and empire of Solomon, have gone the way of all the earth, but the Old Testament has been preserved for the inspiration of mankind. The ark of the covenant and the seven-pronged candlestick have passed from human view; the inhabitants of Judea have been dispersed to the ends of the earth, but the New Testament has survived and increased in its influence among men. The glory of Athens and Sparta, the grandeur of the Imperial City, are a long-lost memory, but the poetry of Homer and Virgil, the oratory of Demosthenes and Cicero, the philosophy of Plato and Aristotle, abide with us forevermore. Whatever America holds that may be of value to posterity will not pass away."[162]

Two hundred and thirty-six years after ratification, I hold it that liberty is the most valuable thing America could ever offer to posterity, and we must protect it. Yes, the Constitution is imperfect, and so is liberty, but "out of our present imperfections, we shall develop that which is more perfect."[163]

---

[162] Calvin Coolidge, Commencement Address, Holy Cross College, June 25, 1919.

[163] Calvin Coolidge, Commencement Address, Holy Cross College, June 25, 1919.

9 798344 928241